ENDURE

Playing Through
Life's Hardest Hits
-An NFL Player's Story

by
Tommie Harris Jr.

ENDURE

Playing Through Life's Hardest Hits-An NFL Player's Story

By: Tommie Harris Jr.
With: Holden Hill

Published by Cedar Gate Publishing
Copyright © 2021 Tommie Harris Jr.

All rights reserved. No part of this book may be reproduced or transmitted in any form or by any means, electronic or mechanical, including photocopying and recording, or by an information storage and retrieval system, without permission in writing from the author.

All rights reserved.
ISBN-13: 978-1736564226

TABLE OF CONTENTS

Foreword

Introduction-The Real Me..................9

Chapter 1-Sudden Change..................11

Chapter 2-Snap..........................21

Chapter 3-Scrambled.....................29

Chapter 4-Who's In Your Huddle?..........39

Chapter 5-Again.........................47

Chapter 6-Training......................59

Chapter 7-Jack and Job..................69

Chapter 8-Morals vs. Morale.............79

Chapter 9-Counterfeit...................87

Chapter 10-Splitting the Double Team.....99

Chapter 11-Enough!.....................107

Chapter 12-Overcomer...................119

Chapter 13-This May Be The Last Time....127

Chapter 14-Resume Your Race............135

Chapter 15-Renewing....................145

Conclusion-If..........................161

FOREWORD

As a speaker, I have traveled around the world, met a ton of people, and heard so many compelling stories. However, I will never forget the day I met Tommie Harris. Getting to know him as a person and hearing his story has been one of the most humbling and exciting experiences of my life. His story, found in this book, *Endure: Playing Through Life's Hardest Hits*, is one of the most heartbreaking, riveting, and inspiring stories I have heard in my career. As someone who was born without limbs, I understand resilience, and I look at Tommie as *my* inspiration to keep pushing when life gets me down.

If you are going through a hard time right now, keep reading and be encouraged to endure whatever life throws at you. When you feel like you don't have the strength go on, when you can't even think about thriving and all you can focus on is surviving, the story in this book has the potential to give you what you need to keep going and play through your circumstances.

I never try to compare brokenness to brokenness, but I've experienced a lot of loss in my life. I've lost loved ones, dreams, and aspirations. Being born without limbs closed so many doors for me, but God used that loss to open exponentially more. By sharing his story, Tommie is allowing God to use his tragic loss to inspire countless others to push through the pain of losing a loved one. If you read carefully and truly connect to his story, you will come away changed.

I am so honored to forward this book, and I look ahead to the impact Tommie Harris, Jr. will make on the world.

-Nick Vujicic

Introduction
THE REAL ME

I heard someone once say, "I am afraid to tell you who I am, because, if I tell you who I am, you may not like who I am, and it's all that I have…"

That's my story.

As an eight-year NFL defensive tackle for the Chicago Bears and three time pro-bowler, I was the best in the world at putting on for crowds and hiding my pain. "Walk it off. And if you can't, then fake it," could have been part of my job description.

I had every luxury life could afford and, as a Christian, I assumed I deserved these "blessings" because I was a good person, good husband, good father, etc,. On all accounts, I was living the dream. Life was easy—until it wasn't.

When my wife passed away from a sudden brain aneurysm in February of 2012, it started a chain reaction of big life hits that God used to challenge everything I thought I knew.

Tragically losing my wife in 2012 taught me more lessons than I can count. Nothing has ever challenged me more in life.

As I went from being on top of the world to feeling like I couldn't walk, I had to learn to stand down on my knees. I learned that you have to breathe if you want to enjoy the run. I learned that once you learn how to endure, you can find joy along the journey again.

Now, I'm learning to make my story bigger than myself.

I didn't write this book to get more fans, followers, or money. I wrote it to allow others like you to step into my shoes and find the same hope I did.

This is the story of God building an overcomer. It's my story, and maybe it will be yours, too. I'm here with you every step of the way!

— TH

An important note:

As you read, you'll find that this book is written according to two different timelines. One timeline occurs after my wife Ashley passed away, and the other occurs before she passed away while I was still playing in the NFL. Every chapter switches back and forth between these two timelines.

Keep an eye out for the distinguishing headers at the top of each chapter, "Cleats On" and "Cleats Off."

Chapter 1
SUDDEN CHANGE
Cleats Off

The world slammed to a standstill around me, melted away, and raced fast as lightning all at the same time. TVs advertised pizza and sunglasses on the airport walls while people flowed around me like water around a stone, all too preoccupied with their phones and travel plans to notice anyone else. And I stood in the middle of it all, baggage claim in front of me, an emotional hurricane roaring inside me. It was February 12, 2012.

"Tommie?"

I blinked, my eyes glossy.

"Tommie, did you hear me? Are you there?"

I remembered the phone limp against my ear.

"What...what do you mean she stopped breathing?"

My wife. Ashley. Sunshine. I had proposed when she came to visit me after my game in San Diego two months ago and we were so excited to get married that we decided just to go down to the Court House and get married there the next day, but we were also planning a large celebration with all our friends in a few months. In preparation for the big day, Ashley opted to finally have a minor breast-reduction surgery that she had been putting off for some time. A common, routine procedure. She was healthy, young, and strong. That's why the words "She stopped breathing" didn't make sense to me.

The voice of the doctor's assistant came over the phone, and I forced myself to listen through my mind's numb haze.

"You're wife...Tommie, I'm so sorry. She experienced a fatal intracranial aneurism while under anesthesia. We have her on life support right now."

I squeezed my phone. I'd been hit in football hundreds of times, I'd experienced dozens of injuries, just two years ago I ripped my hamstring off my pelvis and femur. But nothing in my life to this point came anywhere close to touching the rock bottom pain crawling down my spine. I latched onto the one thing I heard that might give me hope.

"You have her on life support?" I moved past the lump in my throat. My legs felt paralyzed and I wanted to throw up, but I forced my voice to stay controlled.

"Yes. We're keeping her on until you can get here."

With a desperate plea to God, I placed my hope on those final words: "We have her on life support."

"I'm on my way," I said, ending the call and shoving my phone in my pocket. Ditching my coming duffle bag, I jogged to the main airport floor. I ran my fingers over my head as thoughts crashed through my mind.

I talked to Ashley this morning; she was totally fine. She can't be gone. There's no way. She's healthy and strong. It's a fluke, that's all. The hospital doesn't know what they're talking about!

Then, my thoughts spiraled in a million directions.

I've got money. I've got all the money they could ever want or need. I'll spend it all if I have to. Every dime! They have to be able to save her. How much is enough? Whatever it is, I've got it and I'll pay it. Don't worry, Sunshine, I've got this!

After years of succeeding, after a life of achieving, after ten thousand accomplishments, I thought I was capable of anything. I was a lion, I was invisible, I had it all together—and even if I didn't, I always looked like I did. Little did I know just how far I could possibly fall.

I skidded around the corner from baggage claim and scanned the TV monitors for the fastest possible flight to Oklahoma City. Nothing.

I withdrew my phone and fumbled through my wallet for a certain business card. There it was. It belonged to a man I had just met on my flight from Chicago to here in Austin. He was a wealthy businessman who owned a private jet company, and he was an NFL Chicago Bears fan—my team for eight years. We hit it off and he told me with a wink, "Anytime you need a jet, just let me know!" We had laughed then. I wasn't laughing now.

Praying he would answer, I punched in the jet guy's number and hit dial.

"Hello?" came the voice on the other end. I was barely relieved.

"This is Tommie. We met on the flight just earlier?"

"Tommie! Didn't think I'd hear from you again so soon."

I spontaneously knotted my fist and forced myself to take a deep breath, trying to keep my composure.

"I'm sorry, I know we just met a few hours ago, but… if you really meant what you said, I have an emergency and I need your help right now."

"What's wrong?"

"My wife… her surgery went wrong and she's on life support at the Norman Oklahoma University hospital. I need to get to Oklahoma City as fast as possible and there's no commercial flight that will get me there fast enough."

The jet guy's voice grew serious.

"Tommie, I meant exactly what I said. Where are you heading now?"

"I was on my way to see my mom. She lives in Killeen, about forty-five minutes from here."

"Alright. Listen. There's a small regional airport in Killeen called Harker Heights Airport. I'm texting you the address now. Get there as soon as you can, I'll have a jet ready for you when you arrive. Bring your mom if you want. Just tell the pilot your name."

My friend Jarrod was picking me up from the airport. I grabbed my black duffle bag from the baggage claim on the way out of the terminal and looked for Jarrod's silver pickup. I spotted it and quickened my steps.

As I walked, I called my dad. He didn't answer. Next I called my mom. She picked up and I briefly explained what happened. She insisted on coming before I even asked her.

It only took one look at me for Jarod's excited smile to fall from his face.

"What's wrong?" he asked.

"It's Ashley. She's in critical condition at OU Medical Center," I said, stuffing my bags in his back seat and then climbing into the cab.

"What happened?"

"I don't really know. They said she stopped breathing but they have her on life support. Sounds like she will be okay, but I gotta get there now. There's a jet waiting for me and mom at the commuter airport in Heights. You know where I'm talking about?"

Jarod nodded.

Sometimes in life, when we're wondering where God is, it's important to notice the people he's placed right beside us. Jarod was one of those people for me. Sometimes God sends angels into our lives, sometimes he sends people, but he is always present.

About an hour later, Jarod dropped me off at the Killeen/Harker Heights Airport. Mom was already there. She said Dad was on his way. A small terminal sat to our right, and as we walked onto the tarmac, a white private jet purred ready for us.

As we worked our way to the jet, a blue Nissan Titan screeched to a stop on the street outside the tarmac fence. My Dad rolled down his window.

"Tommie!"

I ran toward the fence.

"Dad! Are you not parking? We got to go!"

"For what? She's alright, isn't she?"

"I don't know."

"Don't worry, she gonna be aight. But I got the church folk waiting on me! I'm already late. But wanted to come see you first real quick. I'm putting a prayer up. Hit me when you get there!"

He drove off, and I was left standing on the tarmac. I wanted my Daddy to be with me. I turned around to board the plane, trying to keep it all together. Trying to be okay. But as I reached the jet my strength vanished and I fell to my knees, clawing the hot surface of the tarmac with my fingers.

Gasping between breaths, I began calling on my Heavenly Father. I didn't know what else to do, who else to turn to. Who else could do the impossible?

"God, I need your help… please help me…" I cried under my breath.

My dad was gone, the person I needed the most in that moment.

My mother reached over and held my hand. I remained there for several moments, trying to gather myself. My dad wasn't here, but my heavenly father was, and I began to lean into him.

Ten minutes later, I sat starring out the window at the beams of sunlight piercing the clouds. It almost felt like I could reach out and grab the sunshine. Sunshine, like Ashley. My baby. My wife.

Shaking, alone, and unsure of what awaited me, I prayed, "God, please save her. Please save her. Please save her…"

And if he doesn't?

I clinched my fists.

Like so many Christians in America, I believed in God's power to bring about the outcome I wanted, but I was still learning to trust him to make good out of any situation. I felt I deserved a certain answer from God, and I reminded myself of every reason why things should go the way I wanted.

I was a good Christian.

I treated others with love and respect.

I was a good husband and father.

I gave money to the poor, I used my success to serve those less fortunate than me, and I went out of my way to help others in every way I could.

God had walked with me every step of the way so far, why would he stop now?

And if Ashley is gone, did I leave you?

God's question seemed to burn in my heart. A part of me wanted to surrender, to actually let go, to trust Jesus completely. But how could I?

No matter what, it will be okay, I resolved to myself. *I've got God on my side. I've got connections. I've got all the money in the world. I'm Tommie Harris, for Christ's sake. you got this TH. Next play; this is just like being in a tough game! You always make the big play. Let's go! It's game time!*

I was trying to be all in with my faith, but I knew that if worse came to worst, I had money. I'd seen all the rich people come in before and buy their way out of problems. They buy their kids cancer out, they buy their mom a new heart, they buy their dad's paralysis away—now it was my turn. If God didn't come through, I thought I still could.

Little did I know then, when you put your faith in yourself in life's game, you will always fumble the ball.

The jet landed at the Norman Regional airport, about fifteen minutes from the OU Medical Center. My manager was there to pick me up.

"I'm so sorry, Tommie. I'm so sorry."

I nodded.

"Thank you. Is she doing any better?"

The expression on his face was one I'd never seen before.

"We don't know yet, they are still running tests. But it's not looking good. The doctor said Ashley might have some damage to the brain but they're doing everything they can do and will keep us updated."

Shards of ice crawled up my back.

"But why is she on life support?" I asked, almost begging.

"It's critical, Tommie. But from what I've heard, she may recover."

May recover?

That stood out to me. From all I knew, doctors were running tests and Ashley was going to be fine, not *may* recover.

A feeling started to sink in then that things may be worse than I thought, but I still clung to my hope.

I was ready to fight to the last penny of my NFL fortune to save my wife's life. I believed she might still make it. I had lost football games before, but I had never truly loss someone so close in my life. I always found a way, I always came back stronger, I always made it through. I didn't know how to lose. I didn't think that I could. I wanted to point my own way and I wanted God to help me get there. I didn't want to trust God with *whatever* outcome, I wanted to trust him to deliver the outcome I wanted.

But that's what faith is all about: Letting go of your need for a certain outcome, and trusting God with any outcome.

It's interesting, isn't it? Most of us want God involved in our lives because we think he can help us get what we want, but just in case he doesn't, we choose to still trust ourselves. He's our backup, not our frontrunner. And we don't even realize it. That was me.

When we arrived at the hospital, my legs shook as I stepped out of the vehicle. My whole body felt sick with dread, and it worsened with every step. Finally, we came face to face with the surgeon who had overseen my wife's surgery.

I met his gaze, and I saw the truth in his eyes before his mouth even opened.

"Mr. Harris, I'm so sorry. Your wife had a brain aneurysm we didn't know about. It burst while she was under anesthesia. We are performing tests and we have no signs of brain activity. She's gray matter."

Gray Matter? What does that mean?

"We are preparing feeding tubes for her."

For three days I sat by Ashley's beside praying and fasting for God to make a way for her to come through.

Come on God, make the big play! If you bring Ashley back, you know how many people this will bring to you? God, I never ask you for anything, but this one time do it for me, please God! I'll serve you to the day I die! Please, God!

On the third day, I asked my mother to offer up one of her unstoppable prayers, one with a certified mail stamp on it that gets delivered directly to God's doorstep. God has the power to do anything. He can give life, he can heal, and he can bring back from the grave.

Man, am I gonna have a testimony after this! And I'm in the NFL, too! God, you know how many I'm gonna be able to help now? This is the greatest setup! I'm about to be one of those tried and true saints!

Holding my mom's hand, she began to pray. And as she prayed the machines started to rattle, sounds spewing from every direction, the air started to get warmer, go momma! God's about to do it! Like they say in the old black church, God is about to show up and show out! As mom finished her prayer I sat on the edge of my seat, poised for a miracle. Any moment now.

One minute went by. Tears fell from my eyes as I believed against the odds for God to perform a miracle.

Two minutes.

Three minutes.

Eight Minutes.

Ten minutes.

Ashley's body never budged.

The next day, my whole body seemed to crumble into shock as they led me to my wife's bedside. She was still unresponsive.

I left the room to head into the chapel near the end of the hallway where I could still see Ashley's room but have some alone time to talk to God myself. I sat there pouring my eyes out to him for the next thirty minutes. Then the door burst open. It was my manager.

"Have you seen this?"

"Seen what?"

He showed me his phone.

The big, bold letters of a news headline read, "NFL Pro Bowler Tommie Harris' wife dies of a traumatic brain aneurysm."

A lifeless chill settled over my body.

"What the *HELL!*" I yelled, roaring for the doctor. He came through the chapel door moments later.

"Tommie?"

"I just read on the internet that my wife is dead." I said, holding his gaze and demanding an answer.

The doctor's reply still replays in my mind like a bad play in a game that I can't forget.

"I told you she was gray matter the other day."

"What the hell does that mean? You said you were giving her feeding tubes!"

"No! You misunderstood. Gray matter means she is brain dead. We couldn't find any brain activity. Ashley is an organ donor. We were keeping her nurtured for organ harvesting."

"But I've got money! How much you need? You can have it all, just try to do something!"

"Tommie, I'm so sorry. There's nothing we can do. She's gone."

Have ever been in a place so low that you truly wished you had never been born?

I wanted to keep screaming at the doctor and tell him how wrong he was. "Look! She's on life support *right now!* You see her chest rising and falling? Do something! I've got the money!"

But it didn't matter. All the money in the world couldn't undo what God was getting ready to take me through.

I floated my way back over to Ashley's room, passing by the organ receivers of Ashley's donations.

Why Ashley? Why not me?

I held my wife's hand and sobbed, acknowledging for the first time that she was hopelessly gone. They couldn't do anything. She was brain dead. The only reason they waited for me to arrive at the hospital was so I could say goodbye first.

She. Was. Gone.

My legs collapsed and I fell forward, catching myself as my palms slapped against the ground, snot dripping from my open mouth onto the white marble floor. I tried to stifle a sob, and then I couldn't, and then I yelled with every drop of anguish in my heart. When I couldn't yell anymore, I cried as my mom held me.

I spent the next ten minutes alone in the hospital room holding my wife's hand, watching the machine-assisted rise and fall of her chest, and willing her to gasp for her own breath and open her eyes.

"God…dear, God…do you hear me?"

The only sound came off the machines and the only feeling I felt was fear and anguish, but somewhere deeper than cognition, I knew I wasn't alone.

"God…I know you aren't sleeping or on vacation…I know you are here. Let your will be done."

I kissed Ashley lightly on the forehead one last time. Then, with the doctor back in the room, I pulled the plug on her life support.

"God, thank you for the time."

The machines stopped, and with them, the rise and fall of Ashley's chest. My wife was dead. And with her, I felt like I was, too.

At the time, I had no idea how much my journey was truly just beginning. How do you get whole after losing a limb? How do you fix what's been blown to pieces? How do you get back to normal after your wife just died?

What I didn't yet know was what God was going to teach me in the years to come: you'll never be the same again, but you can be new.

Chapter 2
SNAP
Cleats On

I clinched and relaxed my fists in quick succession, both hands hanging low by my hips like a gunslinger ready for the draw. My leather gloves flexed around my fingers. The air was dry and freezing cold and every breath was marked by a cloud of vapor, but that didn't lessen the fire in my belly, or the sweat dripping down my face.

It was the Chicago Bears vs. the Minnesota Vikings in the 13th week of the NFL season, December 3, 2006. I was lined up on the right side of the ball of the defensive line. At 6'3" 295 pounds, I faced off against 6'8" 350-pound offensive tackle Bryant McKinnie, a.k.a. "Big Mac." He dwarfed me, but I didn't care. The way I saw it, we are all the same size when the ball is snapped.

"Blue eighty! Blue eighty!"

The Vikings quarterback Brad Johnson sounded off his cadence, and I locked my gaze onto him.

I started playing football twelve years ago in middle school. In high school, I was moved to varsity to play as a freshman. When I graduated, I was ranked the number one defensive tackle college pick in the nation. I started as a freshman at the University of Oklahoma. Before my three years at OU were up, I was recruited in 2004 as an NFL first round draft pick by the Chicago Bears.

This was my third year with the Bears, and I was utterly unstoppable—a human wrecking ball. If I wasn't making the play

I was disrupting every blocking scheme. I had led the league in sacks for the first four weeks of the season. I had been selected to play in the 2006 NFL Pro Bowl. NFC had named me Player of the Week twice in just three weeks. I had a million dollar Gatorade commercial with Tiger Woods on the Monday that followed. I was up for Defensive Player of the Year. I was on fire. But something nagged at me. Like there was something distasteful about the whole thing.

Sometimes, I caught glimpses of what all the clout was doing to me. It felt good, but from the outside looking in, I didn't like it one bit. I didn't like what it was turning me into. I would say something and everyone would laugh even though I didn't believe it was my best material. I was tired of shaking people's hands who thought they could use me and giving people a fake smile because they were important and could get me places. Ew! I didn't even know these people. I felt fake from my finger tips to my toes, and it made me sick.

Before the Vikings game, I called my mom driving my midnight blue supercharged Range Rover headed to Soldier Field, this had became a part of my pre-game ritual. "Prayer before Playing." The sun was hanging over the stadium at full height. I said, "Mom, I'm tired of it! And I'm about to get even more money and go even bigger after this? I'm so scared. I don't know what I'm turning into. I don't like it."

She'd been praying a long time. She could feel that my soul didn't want to play. She started saying God was going to bless me in this way or that or give me the strength. Finally, I said, "Momma, you don't understand, I'm tired. I just need a break! These people don't give me a break, I'm always being pulled around! If I'm not on the football field I'm at somebody's community thing or I'm being pulled to a hospital to see a kid or I'm being paraded around at some investor's private event. I'm tired of it! I wish God would give me a break!" I was a grown man on paper but a boy in real time.

Mom prayed God would give me the break I needed. In hindsight, maybe that wasn't such a good thing to ask! Be careful what you ask for, as the old saying goes.

The offensive line across from me shuffled their feet in anticipation, and I tensed my muscles back. I was known for jumping the "snap count"—meaning the instant the center snapped the ball, I was already moving. My right foot was planted against the line of scrimmage, my left foot was braced back a ways, my body poised like a mounted gun ready to fire! Excuse my euphemism.

"Set…hut!"

The center snapped the ball back and the entire line of scrimmage exploded into action. I sprung forward with my high school coach's words echoing in my head, "Be an airplane, not a rocket."

Instead of springing off my back foot to run, I moved it a small half step forward, stomping it next to my front foot. Then, the moment my back foot landed, I pushed off and stomped my front foot forward. With this technique, I generated double the power in the same amount of time it takes to take a single, full step.

Receivers blurred past me as I collided with Big Mac. My cleats held fast to the turf as I repeatedly dug in, yelling and pushing with every last drop of strength in my body. For a moment, Big Mac and I stalled in place, and then, just as I saw the quarterback hand the ball off to Chester Taylor, I felt Big Mac's body fall a half step backward. That's all I needed.

Seizing on Big Mac's momentary lapse in momentum, I pushed harder, throwing him another full step in retreat. Then, ducking my head under his right arm, I got him on my right side and made a break for the running back like I had trained to do a thousand times.

As I penetrated the line and went to make the tackle, I inflight adjusted into that good ol' reliable Soldier Field turf and dove for Taylor. Just as I did, my left foot sank into a pothole at the same time I felt my right foot get stomped on by what felt like an ELEPHANT! Big Mac!

Mid-flight, I tried to open my left leg and adjust, but I couldn't. It slipped, and I found myself doing the splits between my flying left leg and pinned right foot. My momentum continued to carry me to the left, my right foot continued to stay planted, and my body continued to stretch between the two forces until finally, ripppp! My hamstring tore off my bone like a piece of lettuce.

Finally, my right foot popped loose with a handful of turf from under McKinnie, and I finished crashing into the running back and slammed him to the ground. Several of my teammates were close behind and dog-piled on the tackle on top of me. That's when I felt the pain, like knives stabbing my knee and slicing up my leg, as each additional player on the dog pile added to the pressure on my hamstring. It ripped more and more and more, until finally the entire muscle was cleaved clean off my pelvis bone and it couldn't rip anymore.

All the while I heard one voice in the back of my head: "There's your break. You asked for it."

It took several moments before my teammates finally managed to get off of me and I was free to moan and quiver on the ground. Urlacher reached his hand down to me and said his famous phrase, "Get up dummy!"

"Stretcher!" someone called out. "Move him down!"

In no more than a couple minutes, they loaded me up on a stretcher and moved me off the field. Talk about feeling disposable. I thought the whole game was going to stop for me. "Tommie Harris is down! Game canceled!" Hardly. I was barely a blip.

My team kept on without me and won, not only crushing one of our biggest rivalry games of the year 23-13 but also clinching the playoff berth. That meant that even if we didn't win a single other game that season, we were headed to the playoffs, regardless. But we did win more games. And as my team continued to charge on, I remained confined to a rehabilitation center, learning to walk again and watching our games on TV.

As my team fought toward and finally landed at the Super Bowl without me, I was constantly tempted to show myself pity, give up, and sulk in my bad luck.

I lost my Gatorade commercial with Tiger Woods.

I lost my shot at "Defensive Player of the Year."

I missed my chance at playing in the Super Bowl, and not just any Super Bowl, but the historic "Soul Bowl"—the first Super Bowl in NFL history that two African American coaches faced off on the biggest stage. On top of that, we didn't win that year, and I knew that if only I had been able to play, NO QUESTION! We would have taken the trophy.

On the big day, I sat on the sideline with my teammate Mike Brown, who was also out for the game, and watched my brothers go to war without me. All I could do was watch. Sideline ticket, but couldn't contribute. The only good thing about being out of the game was that I got front-row seating to one of the world's greatest half-time performances ever: Prince! I was a huge fan.

When the lights dropped, the stadium went wild. A little silhouette rose from beneath the stage, reflecting a monstrous shadow on the back of the Jumbotron. With one stroke to the strings, the intro began with "Purple Rain." As Prince played, rain began to fall from the sky. The irony! Most people think the song is a break up song, but it's not. Only a true Prince fan knows what he's really talking about: when there's blood in the sky. Red + blue = purple. Purple rain pertains to the end of the world, being with the one you love, and letting your faith guide you.

"I never meant to cause you any sorrow, I never meant to cause you any pain, all I want to see is you dancing in that purple rain…" As the rain landed on my skin, I felt every drop of meaning in the song. I didn't know it at the time, but that night I was learning how to dance in my own purple rain.

My knee and hamstring snapped, and so did my life.

The truth is, snaps happen to all of us.

Relationships fray.
Hearts break.
Dreams collapse.

Like an avulsion, we all experience moments where our lives are being torn apart. But are we to do when life snaps?

If I couldn't give my effort in the Super Bowl, then I would make recovery my Super Bowl.

Pain Management

R.I.C.E. is a commonly used acronym in the medical field when dealing with recovery, and a process I grew intimately familiar with in the months following my injury.

The R stands for Rest. Dealing with injuries can be a traumatizing issue, so it is important for the individual to find a healthy place to heal.

The I stands for Ice. This is something you typically want to do immediately after the injury occurs. Icing is effective at reducing pain and swelling in the inflamed area.

The C stands for Compression. In the early stages of the injury, you want to keep it wrapped up. Not so tight that it restricts blood flow, but tight enough that it prevents further swelling.

The E stands for Elevate. Elevating your injury makes blood flow easier as your heart pumps blood up your leg, and then gravity assists as it flows back down into your vitals. This prevents the injury from throbbing.

R.I.C.E. helps mitigate physical pain and aid the process of bodily recovery, but it also helps with mental, emotional, and spiritual pain and recovery.

For me, I found that rest means to steal away and find solitude in a healing environment. Ice means to pay close attention to what's bothering me and give it immediate attention. Compression means to take all that I'm going through and recycle it for good. Elevate means to raise the issues to God, ask him for the courage to get through it, and hand it over to him.

In the wake of my injury, there were days where all I wanted to do was quit. If being out for the season wasn't bad enough, struggling to raise my own leg three inches off the ground sure came closer. If ever a football player had the right to feel sorry for himself and live into everyone else's pity, surely it had to be after tearing your hamstring.

Instead, I fought for a different perspective. What if this wasn't just something I had to *go* through, but something I could *grow* through?

As a defensive tackle, one of the attributes I was most known for was "jumping the snap." The instant before the center snapped the ball back, I was already on the move. I was the best at capitalizing on the snap of the ball. After my knee and hamstring snapped, I started to see that I could—I needed to—make the most of the "snaps" in life, too.

Waking up and having to be helped out of bed every morning is demoralizing when you've spent your whole life tackling people for a living. My pride took a big hit. To combat my human nature telling me it was hopeless, I made up my mind every day: If I couldn't give my effort in the Super Bowl, then I would make recovery my Super Bowl.

I attacked the recovery process like it was summer training. Is training enjoyable? No. Is training easy? No. But if you commit to the process, does training make you better? Yes.

Snaps in life either produce victims or heroes, and while we may never choose them, we will inevitably experience them. In the end, we don't get to decide what happens to us, but we do get to decide what we do in response. How we emerge is a choice.

Rabbi Dr. Abraham Twerski says it best as he describes a lesson we can learn from lobsters:

"A lobster is a soft mushy animal that lives inside of a rigid shell. That rigid shell does not expand. So how can a lobster grow?

"Well, as a lobster grows, that shell becomes very confining. The lobster feels itself under pressure and feels uncomfortable. It goes under a rock formation to protect itself from predatory fish, casts off the shell, and produces a new one. Eventually, as the lobster grows more, that shell also becomes very uncomfortable. Back under the rocks it goes. The lobster repeats this numerous times. The stimulus for the lobster to be able to grow is that it feels uncomfortable!

"Now, if lobsters had doctors, they would never grow. Because as soon as the lobster feels uncomfortable, it would go to the doctor, get a valium or a percocet, and feel fine again! And it would never remove its old shell. So I think that we have to realize that times of stress are also times of growth, and if we use adversity properly, we can grow through adversity."

When we encounter the snaps of life, we have a choice. And we have to remember that things don't get better, we have to get better.

Don't just go through it—*grow* through it.

Chapter 3
SCRAMBLED
Cleats Off

During my years in the NFL, I co-founded a foundation called *Pros for Africa* with the vision of giving pro athletes and high-profile people the opportunity to be part of real-life practical mission work and share their influence with worthy causes on the frontlines of growth in Africa. I had been to Africa five times, once with Ashley, and just three weeks after Ashley's funeral, I was scheduled to go again.

It felt different being back in an airport, my duffle bag hanging from my hand like it had when I had rushed to Jarod's pickup after hearing Ashley stopped breathing. People still scurried about, watching their phones and kids.

I'm good. God's got it sorted. You're good T, you'll be just fine.

Boarding the plane for London, I forced myself to move down the aisle to my window seat, where I collapsed and opened a granola bar. I opened my mouth and raised the bar to my lips, where I stopped. My hands started shaking and my forehead and palms began to sweat. I felt like a thousand tons of rock were crushing me.

In a burst of pain, I dropped the granola bar and I threw myself to the side of my chair, slamming my head into the window and silently screaming with my eyes shut. When the pain in my heart didn't lessen, I croaked a sob through quivering lips and pressed my head against the window. I stayed like that for several minutes, convulsing against the window with stifled cries.

Then I felt a gentle hand on my shoulder.

"Sir, is everything okay?"

I slowly turned to the voice and saw an older woman sitting beside me, her face concerned. I tried to speak—to say, "Thank you, ma'am. Everything's fine," but I couldn't. Instead, I trembled, squeezed my eyes shut against my tears, and leaned into her hand on my shoulder. She didn't pull away. Instead, she leaned in and pulled my head into her lap.

She didn't say a word and neither did I—she just held me, and I cried all the tears I had shut up for the past three weeks since Ashley's funeral all the way to London in a stranger's lap. I learned a lesson that day: when you want to help someone, don't stand over them, get on the same level with them. Match their posture.

As I cried in a stranger's lap, I could still vividly remember every detail of Ashley's funeral. The way her hair framed her face. The way her green dress rested on her skin. The feeling of her hand in mine as I kissed her goodbye one last time.

A hundred conflicting emotions had crashed through my heart that day and had threatened to tear me apart as I led the funeral procession down the church aisle, my wife's body resting peacefully in front of me in the casket carried by six of my closest friends. Several hundred people had sat in the church, all gathered in Ashley's honor. I had forced one foot in front of the other, hands gripping the smooth wooden pews as I floated to my seat, tremors running through my body like earthquake aftershocks.

When we finally reached the front, the fellas set Ashley's casket down and aligned themselves next to her for the duration of the service. Tyson, my three-year-old son, and Tinsley, my six-month-old daughter, sat some rows behind me, giggling and laughing like it was a normal day back in Sunday service. They were still too young to fully understand that their mom was gone.

I was forced to breathe through my open mouth because my nose was too stopped up. My hands trembled. My shoulders shuddered. My mind limped through my sensory input, unable to fully process what I was seeing and hearing.

As I tried to control my trembling body, I felt my dad's hand gently grab my shoulder. He leaned close and said, "You know, it's just scrambled eggs."

I'd heard those words many times before. I knew what they meant, and they cut through my emotional turmoil like lightning in the night. My back straightened. Every time I was in a tough place, Dad told me the same thing:

"You can't unscramble eggs, son. You can't undo what's done. You're either gonna talk about em, or eat em. It's just scrambled eggs."

Just this once, I thought I was finally low enough to get some of Dad's pity. No luck. Yet again the Mighty Soldier, the "no excuses just results" pastor, showed up again. Man, he's tough! No days off!

I knew how to eat scrambled eggs, but what I didn't realize was that I didn't yet know how to digest them, nor how many times I would have to throw them up and re-consume them to finally learn.

Men don't cry, right?

Christians are always fine, right?

NFL pros don't say ouch, do they?

I wanted to scream with pain. I wanted to drop to my knees and cry. I wanted to fall apart. But I didn't know how. As an NFL defensive tackle, your career rides on your ability to hide your weakness. I'd spent my whole life learning to play through pain without giving a hint of it. I knew how to fill people's opinion of me, whether it was coaches, fans, or kids who looked up to me. I knew how to perform. I didn't know how to fall down, or that there are times you need to.

"Tommie, we're so sorry," friends said with breaking voices.

"It's okay," I'd say back, giving them a big hug and smile. "I'm so blessed for the time I had with her. Every one of us are so blessed."

They'd say, "Our heart breaks for you, Tommie. We miss Ashley with you."

I'd say, "We don't have to miss her; she lives on in our hearts and we'll see her again someday! Remember that."

They'd say, "I can't imagine what you're going through."

I'd say, "I'm fine. God's good through it all!"

The words I said were true, but I was wrong.

That was three weeks ago. Now, on my way to Gulu, Uganda, lying in a stranger's lap on our descent to the London Heathrow airport, I cried out the first of the tears I had suppressed for the past three weeks. There were many more to come, but these were the first.

When I arrived in Gulu, I managed to leave my pain behind on the plane. I breathed in the air. It felt like an escape. I remembered back to March 2006, the first time I came to Africa with the Sunshine Foundation. I'd seen boys parading a cooked monkey down the streets of Monrovia Liberia in a wheelbarrow and selling strips of meat off of it like pieces of beef jerky. Nothing lets you know you're in Africa quite like that.

My trip lasted two weeks. I shoveled dirt, carried pipes, planted water wells, and helped build buildings. I told myself I was there to help others. Maybe I was a little bit. But if I was honest with myself, more than helping others I was trying to bandage my own wounds.

Answering the Tough Questions

In May, two months after Ashley's funeral, I went to Tampa, Florida for training with the Buccaneers. They were considering offering me—and I thought I was ready to try out for—a new playing opportunity.

I wasn't.

I cried the whole flight there, which drained my energy, and then, from the moment drills started with the Buccaneers all the way to the end, I cried as well. Haunting thoughts frequented my head the whole time. I couldn't shake the worry I had about Tyson and Tinsley. Are they okay? Is Tinsley sad? Are they being treated right? If only the tryouts had included a race for racing thoughts!

For the first time in my life, I performed terribly. I literally stunk the field up. Not surprisingly, the Buccaneers turned me down.

Realizing how much my mental state had to do with my physical performance, and also determined to be present with my two kids as much as a father could, I decided it was time to hang up the cleats. My life felt like a bird that just got shot off the sky. But I still refused to let on that I was struggling, even to myself.

My whole life I'd fought to have what I wanted. There was nothing I couldn't do. Play D1 college? Did it. Play in the NFL? Made it. Have millions? Done it. Raise beautiful kids? Raising them. Marry the girl of my dreams? Gorgeous, done! But I guess a part of me still felt like I had to look like I was perfect even when I wasn't.

The months following Ashley's passing were a battle for the right perspective. Was I supposed to be strong? Was I supposed to suck it up and keep going? Was I supposed to withdraw from the world? Was it like a football injury that I was supposed to walk off and pretend didn't happen?

I find that a lot of people in the aftermath of serious loss and grief don't know how to be real. In this, I learned a lot from my son.

Tyson was too young to fully understand what was going on, but not so young that he was totally ignorant. More than once he asked, "Where's mommy?" as if the answer might eventually change if he asked enough times. But the answer didn't change.

"Mommy's with God," I'd say.

"Is she coming back?" he'd want to know.

"She's staying."

"Then can we go there?"

I'd hold him tight, heart pulled in by his childhood vulnerability.

"I want to… but not yet, bubba."

One night, after laying Tinsley down to bed, Tyson and I stayed up. He was three and sat slumped against his headboard, hand holding his favorite stuffed animal his mother got him.

"Tyson…" I whispered, daring to break the silence. Tyson looked up at me.

"Daddy?"

"Come here," I said, reaching out my arm. Tyson crawled against me.

"Tyson…You may not understand me, but I'm going to keep talking to you until you do. Daddy's scared…Daddy doesn't know what he's doing. But I want you to know, I promise you, I'll never let anything happen to you."

I picked Tyson up and carried him to the couch in the theater room where we sat for a long time. Then, without turning or moving, Tyson asked a question that rocked my heart.

"Did Jesus kill mommy?"

Those four gentle words echoed in my head like the crack of lightning. I tried to answer, to make sense of the question, to say something wise and clever. Instead, I stared quietly at nothing as those words rushed through my body. Beneath all my learned behavior, all my theology, all my rationale, all my maturity, and all my image, that one question hit me. The real me. The part of me that asked the same question, but wouldn't acknowledge it.

"No. No, Tyson. Who told you that?"

Tyson shrugged, still laying against my chest.

"Nobody. I just…I know mommy died, and Jesus…that's what he wanted."

I held Tyson tighter, amazed just to hear the question. The *real* question. He wasn't old enough yet to say it right. From the time we're kids in kindergarten, we're taught how to think correctly. In church, we're taught to say, "Yeah, my wife died, but praise God for all his blessings and things are good! I'm just fine." Yeah, right.

I didn't know how to be real. I was an eight year so-called NFL celebrity. I was a performer and had been everyday of my life since high school. That's what I was great at and all I thought I could do. Like so many others, I didn't know how to fall apart. All I knew was how to act like I had it all together. The old saying "fake it till you make it" was becoming my new life's anthem.

Tyson didn't know any of that. He just said, "Did Jesus kill…?"

"No, Jesus didn't kill mommy. Mommy finished running. But she's not gone. Mommy's here," I said, placing my hand over Tyson's heart. "She lives in all of us day to day. As we breathe we share her energy, her life. The way you laugh? She's here. The way you roll your eyes? She's here. The sweets you like? She's here. Your heart? She's here. Mommy ain't going nowhere. She left a part of herself in all of us. And we're going to keep on going until we're finished and we're back with mommy."

Tyson hugged me tighter and I held him, gently rubbing his back in circles. We stayed like that for a long time, holding each other, father and son supporting one another. Finally, I picked Tyson up and carried him to his bed. As I laid him down, he stirred and looked up at me.

"Daddy, who rubs God's back when he's sad?"

I looked at him in wonder again.

"I don't know. That's a good question, bubba. But I do know he cries with us when we're sad."

"Are you sad?"

I looked at my son, and he looked back at me. For a long time we held each other's gaze, and as I looked at him, I saw the face of a child with more faith in adversity than me, and I understood why Jesus said we must become like little children to enter his kingdom. Only the heart of a child can access God-like faith, God-like meekness, God-like vulnerability. God seeks a gleeful childlike heart.

Slowly, tears welled up in my eyes, and as I began to show Tyson that real men cry, so did he.

"Let's pray while crying," I said, pulling Tyson close.

Lord, I want to be real. This is scary. How do I do this, God?

A thought rang through my head: "Just like you worked your butt off to become great at football, dedicate yourself to becoming better at things you know you aren't good at."

How do you be real? My son was teaching me. Real men cry. Real men don't have to keep it all together. Real men lean on others. Yeah, I've heard those phrases my whole life, but putting it into practice was going to take me some time to unlearn my past behaviors. Albert Einstein said it best: "We cannot solve our problems with the same thinking we used when we created them."

Recognize It

After the 2008 Super Bowl, I was honored to be one of three NFL players selected by the United States soldiers to visit the Army hospitals and bases in Afghanistan with the USO Tour. Talk about feeling unworthy. I was getting to meet soldiers who had just returned fresh from battle. They were wounded, torn apart, and wrought with pain.

One man in particular is seared into my memory.

His platoon was hit by a series of IEDs. One of the tanks flipped three times, killing everyone except him. The entire left side of his body was raw, scorched flesh, nerve endings and blood vessels fully exposed.

And he was just one of many.

The hospital was full of trained and disciplined soldiers lying in beds, helpless, all lined up next to each other like in old war movies, awaiting the decision on whether or not their wounds were bad enough for them to go home. The General had the final say as he presented some soldiers with medals.

"How do you feel?" he would ask.

I was dumbfounded. *What do you mean "How do you feel?" He was just hit by a bomb!*

Each soldier fixed their jaw and uttered what sounded like rehearsed cadences.

"I'm good, sir! God's good! Everything's good!"

"Had better days but I'm still here!"

"When can I get back out there?"

Wow. Today, it makes me wonder, when we're in pain, where can we go to say OUCH?

You can get so good at denying your pain that you fail to heal from it. You keep saying, "I'm straight, I'm good, don't worry about me." But, bro! Your arm is blown off and you're leaking blood! "I'm good," you keep saying. But the evidence says brotha, sista, no, you're not.

I saw this all the time in football when a player got concussed. A guy would take a violent hit but insist he was okay. Then I'd watch him walk to the wrong huddle, or I'd watch him ask for water, open his mouth to drink, and pour the water on his head.

When you're wounded or concussed, you don't just "move on." First, you have to heal. And in order to heal, you first have to "deal." You have to recognize you got hit. You have to "deal to heal."

That's the first step in being real: learning to deal with it. Whatever your "it" is. Peace only comes when you commit to deal with your broken pieces, not bury them.

But it took me a long time to learn that.

The moment I pulled my wife's plug, I was so good at performing—at putting on—that it's almost like I couldn't be what I really felt. For me, it was like getting hit in a football game. It didn't matter how bad my body hurt as long as I was still fooling the cameras. Did everybody else think I was fine? Yes? Good. Then just keep up the look long enough for my body to recover.

in order to heal, you first have to "deal."

The problem is, there are some things you don't recover from until you deal with them. You can keep the image up until your injury finally takes its toll and your muscles lock up mid stride, your mind trips a breaker, your vision blacks out, and you crash into a heap on the side of the field.

The same goes for life.

I was mad, I was angry, I was hurt, but I had to be an example. I had to put on for the cameras. Fans were watching me, kids looked up to me, friends were betting on me, and my family was counting on me. So, I kept putting on. I kept encouraging people, being positive, and helping everyone heal—everyone but me. I was pouring out with nothing in me to pour. A vehicle needs oil to keep its moving parts lubricated and running smoothly, or it overheats. I was revving my engine at full throttle long after all the oil was spilled and dried.

It wasn't until the cameras turned off that I started to recognize I was hurting. After my stadium was empty and I no longer had to act like a superhero.

That's when everything began to fall apart.

Chapter 4
WHO'S IN YOUR HUDDLE?

Cleats On

When I played in the NFL, they said I had the fastest get-off of any defensive tackle. No one exploded as fast as me at the snap of the ball, nor target and penetrate the line as fast as me, nor react to the developing play as fast as me. The truth is, they got it partially right. I was certainly fast, but more importantly, I studied film and I knew how to read lips.

I've always loved "film study"—rewatching past games to learn from your mistakes, collect good ideas, and understand your opponents better. It was my secret weapon. I studied my opponents all day and all night, searching for keys to their playing style until finally, "Boom!" I got one. It made me feel like a detective looking for clues at a crime scene. Football is all about paying attention to the details.

At the start of each play, the opposing quarterback would call a huddle to assign the play call and deliver the game plan, and I would pay close attention both during and after the huddle. My film study for the Bears vs. Saints showed me that whenever the great Drew Brees barked out "Kill! Kill!" during his cadence, the play was being changed from a pass play to a run play.

I especially loved playing Steve Hutchison with the Minnesota Vikings. I averaged at least one or two sacks every time we played them because I knew one of Steve's idiosyncrasies. Every time the snap was "on 1" he would shake his fingers, and if it was a hard count, his big white gloves would go as stiff as the Statue of Liberty.

My favorite part of studying film was reporting my nightly findings back to my Defense in the morning. Some guys would listen, some wouldn't, especially if they couldn't see what I saw. I learned later in my career that studying film was different than watching film. Watching film was something the young players were more likely to do. Studying film was something the greats did when studying their opponents.

If I read a quarterback's lips say, "On 1" after leaving the huddle, I knew they were moving on 1. If they said "On 2, on 2!," I knew. As long as the quarterback held a sloppy huddle, I could always read their lips and that afforded me a huge advantage: I always knew the snap count.

That was one of the biggest differences I noticed between rookie and veteran quarterbacks: rookie huddles were loose while veteran huddles were tight.

Rookies would hide their huddles for the first quarter, but when the game started to take its toll and the offense would start wearing down, the strength of the huddle would deteriorate like an onion being peeled. At some point in the third or fourth quarter, they'd give up huddling all together. They'd start yelling their plays out across the field because they were too tired to pay attention to us anymore and so they started thinking we were too tired to pay attention to them. We weren't. We were still listening. And they were just straight telling us their plays.

We'd shrug and receive it. "All right."

Rookies play for short spurts, but veterans play the whole game. Rookies want to win fast, veterans want to win in the end. Veterans have endurance. That's why two teams can go neck and neck for three quarters, but in the fourth quarter, one of them beats the other. Not because they suddenly got better, but because one wanted it more than the other. The winner had endurance, and the other team didn't. They had the ability to see it through no matter what.

Tom Brady and Peyton Manning were savvy veterans.

Every single huddle, they surrounded themselves with their team like building a fortress. It didn't matter whether it was the first play of the game or the last, whether they were winning or losing, whether it was a guaranteed win or the game was hopeless—they *never* let a crack in the huddle. Nothing they did in that huddle ever leaked. They kept their huddle tight every quarter, and as a result, kept their team sharp every play.

Who's in your huddle is important. One sloppy person will not only cause your huddle to leak, but will cause your entire team's performance to drop.

As a defensive tackle, I had to be able to count on my brothers to do their job well.

Tank Johnson was my draft buddy for the Chicago Bears in 2004. I was a first round draft, he was a 2nd round. He was a bulldozer of strength on and off the field and was one of the smartest men I knew. He challenged me everyday and constantly reminded me that I couldn't afford a day off. He was good, and by rubbing shoulders with him, I was challenged to better myself everyday.

Lance Briggs was a hammer and always kept us contained. His job was not to let things spill over. He would make sure nothing broke beyond the first line of defense.

Brian Urlacher kept everyone in order and called the defensive plays and changes during the game. He was our orchestrator.

Mike Brown was one of the hardest hitting players on the field. He was wise as a serpent. As a safety, it was Mike's job to patrol the whole field, cover the backend of the Defense, and destroy anyone who got past us. Mike allowed the defensive line to focus on the job in front of us rather than on worrying about what was going on behind us.

Charles "Peanut" Tillman made things happen. We called him NUT. With NUT on the field, the game was never over. He was our fighter and it didn't matter how much we were down or up, NUT always fought to the end. And that compelled the rest of us to fight with him.

Spice Adam always brought things back down to earth with humor and humility. During the hard times in a game or after a difficult loss, he knew how to restore laughter and hope. In success, he kept us grounded with modesty and hard work. Everyone needs a friend like Spice who reminds you that there's more to life than what's happening to you, either good or bad.

Just like the huddle in football determines the strength you play with, so does your huddle in *life*.

Imagine what your life would be if you were intentional about the people you went onto life's field with? We could have a good person here, have a brother there who's solid, a sister there who will have our back. We could live life in the company of a strong huddle and be ready to perform better than we ever could alone. Likewise, if we have a weak huddle in life, we are doing ourselves a disservice.

I didn't learn what a real huddle was until after football.

When Ashley passed away and I withdrew from my NFL career, most of the people I thought were my friends fell away, too. That's when I learned that life has a huddle as much as football, and that when someone is playing out of position, you have to address it.

In football, it's up to the quarterback to make changes, decide when someone needs a break, and to call out who's not giving their all. In life, we are the quarterbacks; we have full discretion over our own huddles. If changes are not made and cuts are not decided, we will continue to get hit harder, more often, and the damage will last longer. We will have no one to cover for us and no one to help us back up when attacks come.

In life, we are the quarterbacks; we have full discretion over our own huddles.

A strong huddle is not just important for winning football games, but winning in the game of life. My father would always say, "Tommie, you hang around trash long enough, you'll soon start smelling like it."

I started making cuts and changes in my huddle, surrounding myself with people who would be there for me and I could depend on, and people that I knew were in the fight with me. People like Vince Carter, who's been a friend of mine since college and is one of the closest brothers I could ask for. I know Vince is always there for me and is willing to call me out, and because of that, I can trust him to cover me in life.

Who's around you? Who's covering you when you're going for that big play? When you take a risk and jump for these hopes and dreams? Who's covering you? You get to decide. The game of life is inevitable, but your huddle is a choice. You get to choose the people you surround yourself with.

Remember as you choose your huddle in life, the game doesn't change, but the fields do. There will still be double teams, pass interferences, offsides, holding, blindsides, delay of game, timeouts, injuries, and more. These calls will constantly continue in life, which is why your huddle is so important. You cannot predict the conditions of every playing field, but you can prepare yourself and your huddle for any field.

Mentor

Reggie White taught me about one more person you need in your huddle: a mentor. Reggie was my hero.

Today, they would have called Reggie White the GOAT. He was a multi super bowl champ, NFL sack leader, author, actor, preacher, and overall legend. To me, Reggie was my black stallion riding through the night to help the poor and oppressed, he was my lion of Judah roaring for righteousness, he was my example, my teacher, one of the greatest men I've ever met. He modeled the way. The greatest lesson I learned from Reggie was that only what you do for Christ will last.

I remember my first time meeting Reggie when I was a sophomore in college. A couple of friends and I were invited to hear him speak at a Church in Oklahoma City. For me, that was like having a chance to hear Moses speak, just minus the stuttering. Reggie was a fearless leader for Christ. He took his time as he spoke and every word felt like fire and brimstone. He was the real deal.

After he finished speaking my friends and I were asked if we would like to join him for lunch. They said he would like to talk to us.

Lunch with Reggie White?!

"Absolutely!" I replied. This man was my childhood favorite. As a kid, I wore his cleats in high school, watched his movie "Reggie's Prayer" every chance I got, and read all his books. My favorite book of his was "In the Trenches." I wanted to be just like this man! His offer for lunch was huge.

Leaving the Church, they said, "When you get in your car, just follow us."

Follow reggie white? No problem.

The whole way there, I felt like what I imagine a woman feels like as she's getting ready for her dream date Lol! I was so excited.

We pulled up to a beautiful country club and there was a huge buffet laid out as we entered the room. I had never seen that much food before in my life, let alone this kind of food. Some of the dishes I couldn't even pronounce. But I continued on like I belonged, rehearsing what I'd been taught growing up: "act like you've been there before."

I began working my way through the Buffet line, which was much different than the Golden Corral my family and I always went to after Sunday service growing up. This was on another level. Shrimp, salmon, crab. It went on and on. I went in, filling my plate till it looked like a snow cone with everything I could see.

Hey, I'm from Texas y'all and I was a sophomore in college—don't judge me.

I arrived back to the table and placed my napkin over my lap like I knew to do at fancy restaurants. Grabbing my knife and fork, I bit into one of the shrimps and let my mouth go crazy.

Soooo good.

Then suddenly, my trance was broken as my plate was swept away from me like it got caught in the wind.

Wait! What? Where's my plate going!

All I could see was a huge black hand reaching over my shoulder. I looked up. It was Reggie White.

"We don't eat that!" he exclaimed.

"Eat what?"

"Real men don't eat shellfish," he said.

I zipped my mouth shut, dumb founded and lost for words.

Wait, what? Okay. I guess if it makes you that mad, I won't eat shellfish anymore, I thought to myself as I tried not to laugh.

That was my first mentoring experience with Reggie White. He was beginning to teach me what he had learned on his life journey so far.

He taught me hundreds of lessons throughout my life.

"A good leader doesn't sit back and let you fail, they make you better."

"A real man does't sit back and watch things happen, they make things happen."

"Real leaders don't sit back and react, they attack."

That day Reggie pulled my plate away from me was the day I felt like I joined the Reggie White huddle. I committed myself to being in the trenches with him. I was in great company.

You know the saying, "Show me your friends and I'll show you your future?" Well, following a man like Reggie White, I knew my future was strong.

The company you keep will determine how far you truly go. In the words of my father, "You hang around trash long enough, you start smelling like it." No game can be played without a strong huddle, and no huddle can stay strong without mentors pouring into you.

Every great huddle in life's game should be built up of quality men and women with great character. My question for you is, who's in your huddle? Write down the people around you who make your huddle stronger and the ones who weaken it. The ones who weaken your huddle need to be cut. They won't make the next season's team.

And all great leaders should remember this: unless someone is eating shellfish, make sure you ask them if they're finished eating before taking their plate!

Chapter 5
AGAIN
Cleats Off

"Mr. Harris, you're up next in five minutes!"

Sitting backstage at the TBN broadcasting center, I worked to control my nerves. My stomach was spinning like clothes in a washing machine, my knees wouldn't stop shaking, and sweat soaked through the fabric of my dress shirt. In five minutes, I was going to be on a stage in front of hundreds of thousands of viewers.

As I worked to prepare myself for this broadcast, I flashed back to my childhood thinking, and how I faced challenges back then.

"God, make me bold like Bishop Thomas." Bishop Thomas was a senior pastor at the church I was raised in. I'd been praying this since I was a kid, which I guess can tell you what crowd I hung out with. The holy crew. Sunday morning church, Monday night service, Tuesday night prayer meeting, Wednesday night YPWW (Young People Willing Workers), Thursday night outreach event, and last but not least, Friday night joy night, my favorite. I had Saturdays off.

The term churchy was an understatement.

Growing up saturated in church had its positives and negatives. Some positives were the assurance that I was never alone or too far gone for God's love and learning to focus my life on loving and serving others. Negatives included finding my self-worth in how well people thought of me and thinking I was better than others. Mind you, these weren't negatives of *following Jesus*—of that, there are no negatives—but instead were reverberations of being ultra submerged in American church culture.

With that upbringing, I've always admired pastors, preachers, and speakers who were "men of God" and possessed the "anointing" that made others feel encouraged, inspired, and comforted by merely being in their presence. I loved the way the power of God rolled from their lips.

Over the years, Bishop Thomas went through a number of personal troubles. He decided to *grow* in the process and allow others to learn from his living story as he overcame his obstacles. Like Bishop Thomas, I too wanted a testimony that could touch others' lives.

As they say, be careful what you ask for.

After losing Ashley, my life turned upside down. Like Bishop Thomas, I was on my way to having an "overcomer" story as well. "What did this mean?" I wondered.

What if I didn't have to just endure my story; what if I could use it?

I've found that our stories can often be the key to unlock another person from their pain. Not only is it healing for us to share it, but it is powerful for another person to hear. We can't bury our key.

I'd always been inspired by motivational speakers like John Maxwell, who always made the crowd feel welcome in his presence, or Tony Robbins, who gave strategy in the face of hopelessness, or Les Brown, who commanded the room like a general of peace. These were men who shared their key. I soaked in their words and was inspired not only by what they said, but also to follow in their footsteps. What if I could become a motivational speaker?

I made the decision to invest time and money in training myself as a speaker and learning how to tell my own story in hopes of one day becoming like those amazing examples. Now, as I prepared to go on stage on TBN, I had an opportunity to put my speaking into practice.

Like many others, I'd been through the ringer and was in the process of overcoming, and boy, did I have a story to tell!

This is just like coming out of the tunnel, T....

"Would you please join me around the world in welcoming brother Tommie Harris!"

TBN's recording studio in New York roared in applause, and I shook the hand of Pastor Smokie Norful before taking a seat. Smokie was a Grammy Award-winning gospel singer and pianist.

Several months prior, Smokie called me to say he was going to be hosting a special Christmas edition of TBN, the largest Christian broadcasting network in the world. He was bringing several guests into New York City for his show and was hoping I would be one of them. If I was ready, he was offering me the opportunity to discuss my new Locker Room campaign and share my story publicly for the first time. The Locker Room was devoted to helping build fellowship groups for men across the country and providing them with a place where they can admit their pain and start to heal from it.

As it was, I couldn't wait.

"Bless you man! Thank you for being here today. Now, the world knows you as a former NFL player, but," Smokie grinned here and continued with a friendly jab in his voice, "what they don't know is that you're also an incredible psalmist."

The crowd seemed to lean in at that moment. I couldn't help smiling sheepishly. I had written several poems and songs over the years and a few particular ones since Ashley's passing, but I wasn't secure enough in my singing or writing skills to share them in public yet.

"Well, I do a little bit, but I'm not about to sing after you just slayed the stage up here!" I jabbed back. Smokie had just obliterated the mic singing one of my favorite songs "I Need You Now," one of his many hits. We laughed. Maybe someday I'd sing for people, but not yet.

My nerves made themselves known. The bits of doubt I was feeling began to roar.

I don't belong here...I'm not ready for this...What was I thinking?

Fear rushed through me. I looked at Smokie, wishing he knew how much I needed him to put his hand on my shoulder or give me a short word of encouragement or a wink that said, "You got this"—anything! Something to tell me I wasn't alone. I felt like a kid who'd lost his parents in a large crowd.

I wanted to cry out, "Daddy, where are you? I need you NOW!" Instead, I did the only thing I knew how to do in uncomfortable situations of fear and doubt. I took a deep inhale, then exhaled slowly. My dad wasn't here, but my Father in Heaven was.

What would you do if you weren't afraid, T? I asked myself. *What can God not do?*

"Now, the word tells us we overcome the accuser by the blood of the lamb and the word of our testimony," Smokie said, steering the conversation in a new direction. "And there's an incredible testimony in you. Two months after getting married, you lost your wife tragically."

I nodded. "Yes, Sir."

"And you guys had children," Smokie continued.

Again, I nodded and said yes, Sir.

"So, tell me, how has your faith held you, kept you, and helped you navigate such an awesome loss in your life?"

I looked at Smokie. And as the words started coming out of my mouth, I remembered everything.

It was three years after Ashley's passing. In the aftermath of Ashley's death I had decided to retire from football in order to focus fully on being a father. Tyson and Tinsley were goofballs and both going to school now, and six months ago, I'd gone back to school myself to finish my MBA from the University of Miami. I still loved my Sooners, but Miami felt right to me if I was going to pursue being an inspirational speaker and "God-treprenuer."

Life was finally starting to feel slightly normal again, but it wasn't without its challenges.

As for the kids, Tyson and Tinsley dealt with their own share of issues: bullying at school, putting up with kids making taunting remarks throughout the year and on Mother's Day.

"What are you going to do with your momma today?" classmates would ask, knowing full well that Tyson and Tinsley didn't have a momma. Kids can be brutal. I told Tyson, "Next time someone says something about your momma, you tell them, 'My momma finished her race, yours still has to finish hers.'"

On my side, my challenges were far more hidden. Still ignoring the gaping wound in my heart, I walked through life like everything was fine. It would take a long time and a whole lot more pressure for me to finally acknowledge differently—that I was hurt.

That's why I was here on stage at TBN today. I'd convinced myself I was fine. I was here to help others. Which maybe I would. But the one who needed my attention the most was me, likely because I was the one I neglected the most. I was doing the only thing I knew to do.

Help others. God's got it. What would you do if you weren't afraid?

"First off, let me say that in my life, I was always the best. Number one draft. Number one at Oklahoma University. Number one at everything. So my whole life, I was never really tested. I knew God in a good place. I didn't know him when things didn't go the way I wanted them to."

The crowd sighed in understanding.

"I would always ask God when I was in college, 'God, this is how I want to know you: I want to be able to walk into a room and have people really feel the anointing of God. But you gotta be careful what you ask for! By no means am I perfect, but every day, I wake up with a quenching for God like, 'What do you desire for me?'" I continued to tell my story.

"My wife went to have breast reduction surgery in Oklahoma. She was doing it for Valentine's Day and getting ready for our big wedding in July. We were married on January first in a private ceremony but were looking forward to something more public in the summer. I was playing in San Diego, and God told me 'Why don't you just marry this woman?' You know, when you're a man and you're going through a relationship, everybody's telling you this and that about love. And it kinda makes you drag your feet a little bit! I remember Ashley flying down to come visit me in San Diego where I was playing, and I said, 'Let's just get married. Let's go down to the courthouse and get married!' And we got married on New Years.

"After that, she went to get a breast reduction to fit her little dress—she wanted to look good for the wedding on July 9th. And when she called me, she said, 'Come down to Oklahoma afterward! We're gonna go out, we're gonna have a blast!' So I'm on my way to go meet her, and I find out that she's unresponsive. And I'm confused, it's just a breast reduction, she should be in and out. She ended up having a brain aneurysm.

"At that moment, when I got the news, I remember God asking me a simple question, 'Do you trust me?' And in that moment as tears began to run down my face, every tear meant something to me, and every tear began to speak to God. I remember kneeling on my knees asking God, 'I want to be like Bishop Thomas! God, I wanna know you in another way!' And the words 'Do you trust me?' played like a melody in my mind. And every tear made sense, like, don't panic. Trust in God. And from that point on, my whole desire in life was to show people to appreciate breath.

"At twenty-eight, I pulled the cord on my wife. I had to decide, is she going to just exist in a vegetative state, or should I let her go on? And God said, 'Let me handle it.' And from that point on I told God, 'I will show people to give their loved ones the flowers while they can smell 'em!'"

The crowd was leaning in and began to clap with agreement.

God, what can you not do… I continued to repeat in my head.

"Don't wait till the battle is over! Don't wait till you're turning over in the casket! But every day we gotta realize we are dying daily, and that the casket gets closer every day. So my whole thing is just to encourage all the believers that God is able to do whatever! He is able to do exceedingly, abundantly above all."

Smokie chimed in then, "Man, it's amazing to me, that when you ask God for increased faith, it comes through the testing of your faith. You know, I say this often, faith is not faith until it's been tested. Until you have to trust in the Lord with *all* of your heart, then completely lean not to your own understanding. Because his ways are not our ways, his thoughts are not our thoughts, as high as the heavens are from the Earth so are the ways of the Lord from us. When you really are in that position where you have nothing else to depend on but God and his word, that's when your faith really becomes faith."

His words pierced me. I felt like I was a nail having a conversation with a hammer on a construction site. "Bear with me," the hammer was saying. "I know it's going to hurt, but only for a little while. I gotta bang on you. It's not personal. You're the last finishing piece for this house to be completed."

What would you do if you weren't afraid? I reminded myself again.

I received Smokie's words and let them minister to my heart. I was under construction.

"And what you're saying means so much to me now," I said. "I can understand. You know, when you haven't been tested, you just hear these words. But when you've gone through *something*, when you've gone through something! You understand a little more.

I'm here to encourage everyone, in the dark times, we've been made to *endure*. And to endure. And to endure. My message to all the people of God is to know how to prepare for these struggles. We need to be prepared for these things to come. We've been made to endure the night, but the joy comes in the morning!"

The crowd resonated with cheers, and as I shouted the words, I was actually encouraging myself to endure through my mournings.

"So that's what it is! I'm going to keep going and going and going until the morning comes! I'm going to keep going for God."

"Let's talk about the preparation," Smokie said. "You said we need to prepare. What are the best methods of preparation? We know that in this life we will have tribulation. So how do we prepare for that?"

"I think that preparing is admitting the truth," I said. "I was talking to a friend on the way here, and I said it's crazy how we laugh at alcoholics who get enough courage to go admit they're alcoholics. We laugh at drug addicts who admit they have a drug problem. But we're the same people who sit and laugh at these people who struggle with the same situation *we* are dealing with! And we just have to start admitting, God, I'm not all that I pretend to be! I'm broken, too! If you can admit it, that's when God can begin to grow you!"

As I listened to my own words, I called into question my own pride. Was I refusing to admit my own wounds? Was I refusing to be vulnerable? I didn't know. More truthfully, I didn't want to know, and I moved my thoughts along before they uncovered anything I didn't want to deal with.

Smokie jumped in.

"True repentance."

"That's it," I agreed.

"True repentance leads to God's forgiveness and total restoration."

"Yes, Sir."

"Now, following your wife's passing, you left the NFL. What prompted you to do that?"

"Well, actually, I didn't leave the NFL, it's kinda like the doors were locked on me. I'm so glad that it happened though. I'm learning so much. It's painful, but it's necessary. I'm so serious. I tell God, whatever you need to do… *Whatever!*"

The crowd erupted with agreement.

"If I gotta lose again! In order to do what you need in my life. I didn't pick my name, my skin color, you put me here! I didn't get to pick any of it, so whatever you gotta do in my life, you get the glory!"

God, what can you not do?

The crowd was cheering in uproar by this point. Smokie laughed.

"I gotta warn you, you're on a stage with a pastor."

"I'm sorry now," I joked back.

"You can't raise your voice like that! Cause I'll go with you!"

We laughed together.

"Is there anybody out there who has a 'whatever' kind of faith?" Smokie asked the crowd. People cheered and shot their hands in the air, energized by my story. I watched and I was glad, filled with hope because of what I saw Jesus doing through the tragedy I had fought through. It's amazing how using your story to love others can also bring you healing.

Those words resonated in my heart: "A 'whatever' kind of faith!" I was reminded of what Tony Evans always said: "Faith is acting like it is so even when it's not so believing that it shall be so because God said so."

And then, there was what Smokie had taught me: increased faith comes by the testing of your faith.

Little did I know, my testing was just beginning.

Thalia

The process of healing wasn't clean cut and perfect.

Around the time I started going back to school, I reconnected with my beautiful, intelligent friend Tashia from high school and we started dating. Maybe a year or so later, we were pregnant.

I know that doesn't sound good to the "church crew" and I don't want to send the message that my actions were right, but it's the truth of my story. Anyone who knows me knows that I am a very private person and I would have rather written a book where I came out looking good and perfect, but that's not what this book is about.

I'm speaking to the person who finds themselves in sudden circumstances, or has been undetermined, or has been sabotaged, is embarrassed, afraid, or alone, and is wondering, "How did this happen to me? Where did I go wrong?" I want you to know that you are not alone and that there's hope. I'm a living witness. Always remember, you are not performing for men, but for an audience of one.

It's taken me a while to admit I'm not perfect. I've always acted like I had it all figured out. Actually, I've spent many years playing perfect and worrying about what others think. Like Sabrina Hudson, a renowned writer, said, "I'm afraid to show you who I really am because that's all I have and you may not like it." But I'm learning that the only way I am going to "grow through" and not just "go through" is to admit my flaws. You can't look good and heal at the same time.

As David confesses in Psalm 32:3: "For when I kept silent, my bones wasted away through my groaning all day long."

I want to show you who I really am. Please be patient with me, God's not through with me yet. In the words of Rag'n'Bone Man, "I'm human after all, don't put your blame on me."

On February 9, 2016, four years after Ashley passed away, my new, beautiful baby girl was born. Thalia. I was scared of what people would think, but more than that, I was so excited for this new life God had blessed me with.

Around this same time, I invested in several business ventures with some friends. Guys I trusted…but guys I should have stayed away from. More on that later.

I was getting home from my boxing gym and had just finished a business call. It was June 15, 2016. Tashia was an ER doctor and was back at work for the first time since giving birth, and I was doing private off-season boxing training in Georgetown, so we decided to leave Thalia with Tashia's mother.

I threw my keys on the counter and was getting ready to take a shower when my phone started to vibrate. I had grown accustomed to keeping my phone on vibrate since getting that call in February, 2012, and getting the news Ashley stopped breathing. The sound of ringing phones gave me anxiety after that. I was wearing my red and blue training outfit—I remember, because I was looking into the mirror.

And then it happened suddenly.

I picked up my phone and looked at the caller. It was Tashia's mother, who our daughter was staying with. A pang of anxiety flashed through my mind, but I made a conscious effort to dismiss it. I was just being paranoid. Everything was fine.

"Hello?"

"Tommie! The baby's not breathing!"

I froze.

What?

The words of Thalia's grandmother sliced through my phone like a cold knife. They sounded too much like the words of the doctor's assistant four years ago: "Ashley stopped breathing."

Shards of ice shot through my body.

No. Not those words again. Not them. Not now.

"What?" I managed to get out.

Not my baby girl. No. Please, no.

"Tommie, you need to get down to Killeen! The baby's not breathing. The ambulance is here."

As I raced through the back country roads to the hospital, I called Tasha. She was rushing back from Dallas. My knuckles were white on the steering wheel as I drove, terror ripping through my body.

God, please, no!

I arrived at the hospital to see my daughter. I walked in and was led to her room. And then I saw her—her little body covered in a white sheet, her arms stretched out. Gone.

The doctor said the cause was Sudden Infant Death Syndrome (SIDS), which is the diagnosis for around 2,300 infant deaths per year in the United States with no particular illness or cause. It is the third leading cause of infant death in the United States.

Sudden.

Ashley died of a brain aneurysm—sudden. Thalia died of SIDS. Sudden. In the game of life, things can change on a dime.

Sudden things happen suddenly.

As I held my baby girl's hand, so small one of my fingers fit in her whole palm, I asked God in silence, "What are you doing?"

A year and a half ago, I told my friend Smokie on the TBN interview, "I have a *whatever* kind of faith!"

Now, it was time to find out if my words were true.

Chapter 6
TRAINING
Cleats On

One swift cleat after the other, I tore through afternoon summer practice at the University of Oklahoma. Drops of sweat crawled down my face and dripped from my chin as the sun hung heavily in the sky. The field baked with triple-digit heat. I felt like one of those warmed- over dishes sitting under cooking lamps at Golden Corral. Everyone was dragging their feet that day and cutting corners Coach didn't see. We were all tired, and it was easy to get away with average effort. Until Coach finally got fed up.

"Tommie!"

I looked up just in time to get a blast of hot air and spit in my face as my coach, Jackie Shipp, interrupted the drill and yelled down my neck. He was a former NFL linebacker for the Dolphins and Raiders who played eight seasons and at thirty-eight years old he was even bigger and stronger than me. I tried to keep cool.

"What the hell was that?" he demanded.

"What?"

"Your pathetic, sorry-a** effort! That's what! We thought you were the best DT in the country and you are playing like a one star!"

For some reason, he wasn't yelling at everyone else who was performing equally apathetic—just me, the eighteen-year-old freshman from Killeen, Texas.

"It's just practice," I said, unfamiliar with the difference in standards between a five star and a one star.

Coach Shipp grabbed my face mask and leaned his face into mine.

"Shut your trap, freshman. This is not *just practice.* This is training. Do you understand me?" he growled, pelting my face mask with splinters of Copenhagen fine tobacco.

I gritted my teeth. Coach Shipp kept going.

"How you prepare here is how you'll perform out there! We don't fight to make the playoffs or to be runners up. No. We win championships, Son. In order to start on this line, you have to show me you're capable of it! I don't care that you're a five-star recruit if you're acting like a chump. You ain't gon' water down these boys who really want it. We're just coming off a national championship! We can do it again with you or without you, Son! Your choice!"

I tore my helmet off and glared back at Coach Shipp, eyes blazing.

"I'm *not* a—"

"Not a what, Son? An a** chump! Is that what you were going to say, Tommie Harris? Because I don't care what you tell me, I care what you show me on this field!"

"I'm the number one defensive tackle in the country!" I said, firing back. "I've got offers from every single D1 school. I'm the best DT you've got and you know it! You know I'm not a chump!"

"Really? You know, I used to think you were, but I can't tell anymore, Son. You're all talk, talk, talk! That's all you are. All talk and no walk. You ain't doing nothing but running your mouth, Son!"

"You can't talk to me like that!"

"Like what? Like you sitting here wanting somebody to feel sorry for asking you to be what they thought you were? You ain't playing like the Tommie Harris I recruited! Maybe I'll get someone else to fight on my line. I brought you here because I thought you could do it. I believed you could come in and contribute as a freshman, but obviously I was wrong. How's that sound? I'll get somebody else and you can go back home. Than you can pittle and pattle around all you want!"

I tried to keep my bottom lip from trembling as I held Coach's fiery gaze.

"I'm done with this," I said.

"What's that?"

"I said I'm done! I quit! I'm leaving!"

"Oh, yeah? Where are you gonna go?"

"I'll go back to Texas! They wanted me and they'd still love to have me!"

"Yeah? Go on, then. Get the hell off my field and run down to Texas! Just make sure you remember, you quit this team not because I was too hard on you but because you were scared to be great!"

I shuttered under Coach's intensity, trying to keep my composure. I wanted to cry and I hated it. I didn't move.

"Go!" Coach yelled.

I felt my eyes moistening and I rubbed my forearm across my face, trying to bury my emotion. When I still didn't move, Coached snapped his cellphone open and punched in a number. I heard several muted rings, then someone picked up.

"Just a moment, Mrs. Harris," Coach said into the phone, then to me, "Here's your mother, Tommie. Tell her to come get you cause you want to leave."

I looked at Coach for a minute. His eyes drilled me, his outstretched hand unwavering. Finally, I took the phone.

"Mom?"

"Baby? What's wrong?"

"Mom," I blubbered through half sobs, "he was screaming and cussing at me! Coach Shipp he wasn't like that during recruiting. He was calling me names and saying I don't deserve to be on the team! I'm done here momma! I want to come home."

Momma's voice came through.

"Oh, baby! It's okay! You can come home now, baby! Don't worry. I'll be here just as soon as—"

The line clicked as someone else picked up the other phone in the house.

"Janie Bell," said a steady, firm voice, much like Mufasa from The Lion King .On the other receiver—the voice of my father. "Hang up the phone." Janie!

Mom sniffed once more, said we would talk more in a minute, and hung up the phone.

"Tommie, you listening?" my father asked.

I inhaled deeply, trying to steady myself and re-enlist my inner strength. Something is different when a boy's father speaks to him. A boy's mother can love him, nurture him, and believe in him, but only a boy's father can call out the man in him. Male to male. Alpha to alpha. Warrior to warrior. That's what was happening now.

"Yes, Sir, I'm listening," I finally answered.

"Let's get this straight right now: I can tell you the one thing you're *not* going to do is quit."

Those words reached into the furnace of my heart and rekindled the strength I had let falter. The strength of my Father, a disciplined military man, had taught me my whole life. Dad continued.

"We don't quit in our family. That's not an option, so get it out of your head. I don't know what's going on but it sounds to me like you're a little uncomfortable. Let me ask you a question, Son: Does being uncomfortable mean you get to pull out? To retreat?"

"No, Sir."

"Good. Now that we've got that cleared up, you want to tell me what's going on?

I took a deep breath.

"Yeah…Coach Shipp's cussing me out and telling me I don't deserve to be here. I want to go back to Texas. I had committed there a few months ago, they'd kill to have me back."

Dad was quiet for a moment.

"Is Coach Shipp talking to you?" Dad asked.

I knew what he meant.

"Yes."

"I've told you before, I'll tell you again. Don't listen to what he's saying, just know he's talking to you and not at you. Start worrying when he's not talking to you. It ain't coming out the way you want to hear it, but he loves you because he's talking to you." Dad raised his voice and yelled, "I said, don't listen to what he's saying! You hear me? Just know he's talking to you!" Not at you.

"Yes, Sir."

"Good. Now, you gave that man your yes, didn't you?"

"Yes."

"Yes, you did. You sat with your mom and me and you gave that man your word that you will commit and dedicate yourself. You said you're going to Oklahoma. You remember why you chose Oklahoma over every other school in the country, don't you? Every other school offered you to start, but Oklahoma offered you a *shot* at starting. They didn't compromise their integrity in order to buy your talent. You would still have to earn your place, and you liked that."

I remembered. Dad continued.

"We're not going to Texas, Son—Texas is out of the deal. Now, go back out there and do what you committed to do, not what your emotions make you want to do. Go tell Coach Shipp 'Yes, Sir,' shut up and know he's talking to you and not at you, and prove why you should start on this team. You're going to work your butt off like we both know you can. Go be Tommie Harris. You hear me, Son?"

I took another deep breath.

"Yes, Dad."

I locked eyes with Coach Shipp and handed the phone back.

"You good?" Coach asked.

"I'm good."

He nodded, then turned to the rest of the team.

"Alright! Tommie's done pouting. Let's go. Everyone on the bags! I'm tired of the weak energy today. I want ball-get-offs as hard and fast as you can! Tommie, see if you can remind me why you're the best defensive tackle in the country."

And I did. For the next three hours I crashed pads, flung dirt, and whooped butt.

I was learning to fight. To play through the pain and hold on through the discomfort. I didn't like being uncomfortable. In the moment, I wanted someone to pull me out of it.

I'm so grateful Coach Shipp never let it happen. He forced me to fight my own way out of my chrysalis.

Chrysalis

A chrysalis is the hard exoskeleton that a caterpillar forms for the final stage of metamorphosis into a butterfly. When its metamorphosis is complete, the newborn butterfly is weak, vulnerable, and flightless.

"Flightless?! It's a butterfly!" you might think.

Yes, but despite its beautiful new wings, the muscles aren't yet strong enough to flap once, let alone sustain the rate of twenty-beats-per second needed for flight.

"So how does a butterfly ever find its place in the sky?" you may wonder.

The answer is the gift in disguise: breaking free of the chrysalis. The struggle of climbing out of the chrysalis is what strengthens the butterfly's wings. That's why you should never help a butterfly free of its chrysalis. It might look like you're helping it—just take out your pocket knife, open the chrysalis slit a little wider, and the butterfly is free!

Yes, it's free. But free too soon.

Without the struggle, the butterfly will never be able to fly.

Like butterflies, the fight and struggle is what defines your own uniqueness. Never allow someone to cut you out of your process. I was uncomfortable under Jackie Shipp's coaching and wanted out, but my father refused to let me. He knew what I know now: struggle is what it takes to grow. Neither Dad nor Coach Shipp ever let me settle for being a caterpillar when they knew I was to become a butterfly.

During my next three years of playing at the University of Oklahoma, our coaches would occasionally make a training drill out of running up and down the ramps that went to the top of the stadium. They'd stand halfway up the stairs to time us and keep us motivated with their own blend of encouragement and smack talk.

"Look like he tired, Boss!" they'd call after one of our biggest linebackers trucking up the stairs, or, "You don't want to be the best do you? You better run faster or you're coming back!" they'd yell after a tired receiver who just passed by.

Standing halfway up the stadium and spurring on their players, what our coaches never thought about was the elevator at the top of the stadium that went all the way down to the level of the field. With the majority of the team still running up and down the stairs, it was easy to miss the five to ten players at a time who snuck onto the elevator, rode it down, and rejoined the drill at the bottom without our coaches ever noticing.

Every single day we ran those ramps, I was forced to make a choice: do I get better, or do I cheat the drill?

Most of the guys who took that elevator never made it to the NFL, and those who did didn't last long. I chose to become better. The difference between them and me? It wasn't the stairs. Running the stairs instead of taking the elevator occasionally isn't what separated us, it was our mindsets. While their mindset thought only of what was right in front of them, I was playing the long game.

In life, it's tempting to look for the easy way out of situations. It's easier to run from the fear of change and avoid the pain of growth than to face your chrysalis and fight through it. But as long as you run from it, you'll never escape it.

What's on the other side of your chrysalis? And what are you missing out on because you are staying confined in it? Your blessings are on the other side, your courage, your maturity, your growth—the man or woman you have the potential to be! But you have to believe you can make it. If you don't believe it you won't make it through.

Unlike butterflies who undergo the process of a chrysalis once, we as humans undergo chrysalises constantly throughout our lives. Maybe some of yours have looked like mine. Maybe your career fell apart. Maybe you've lost loved ones. Maybe you feel unqualified to be a single parent.

Endurance does not care about other people's opinions.

Whatever your challenges have looked like, we can all relate to this: they keep coming.

Your business is losing money, and then your son is injured in a car crash, and then your mom is diagnosed with cancer, and then, just when you're starting to get back on your feet, another challenge crashes in. But it's in the long game that endurance really manifests.

When you endure, you find that you aren't simply surviving but actually growing. When you press in and allow your chrysalis to *grow* you, the next one seems a little easier, and the one after that easier still. But in truth, nothing got easier, you got stronger. Like John K. Kennedy once said, "Do not pray for easy lives. Pray to be stronger men."

The world may not know the full extent of what you've grown through. People will admire the person you are and say they want to have the strength that you have, and you have to be able to look back at them and smile knowing that, if they only understood what it took to be as strong as you, they may be less eager.

When people watch your journey, remember that it's like going to a boxing match and only watching three rounds. They don't see every time you got hit, they don't see the blood you spit from your mouth, they don't see you when you started, and they haven't seen you every time you've won. They have a limited perspective for understanding how great your victory is or how strong your progress is. But endurance doesn't care about other people's opinions.

While spectators come and go and see glimpses of the fight, endurance is committed to the whole. Yeah, we might be in just this part of our life right now, but we're committed to the whole thing and a single moment does not end us. We know where we've been and we know there's more ahead than anyone else could ever imagine.

When people criticize your journey, tell them, "I'm in the tough part of the game right now. I'm in a tough quarter." The truth is, even though you might be down a little in one quarter, you'll get back up. As long as you've got time on the clock the game isn't over.

That's what endurance is. It keeps you in the long game and locked into the bigger picture. You go from the nail to the shed. The product of a process.

On your journey of struggling through your own chrysalis, I hope you remember that our toughest times and our darkest days are where most of our development takes place. Continue to toil. To labor to exhaustion. You can't see it while you're in it, but the exhausting, uncomfortable thing you're going through is what will fill your wings with unique beauty and strength.

Rather than looking for the easy way out, look for the growth-way out. That's how you learn to fly.

Chapter 7
JACK AND JOB
Cleats Off

My wife was gone. My career was gone. My daughter was gone.

For several weeks, I existed in a distant daze. Externally, I was still "rockstar-Christian" Tommie Harris, but inside, I was crumbling. Every inch of my heart exploded with raw pain and anguish. I felt like I was being physically torn apart. And even though God wasn't causing it, he was letting it happen.

Despite the pain I felt, I refused verbally to lash out at God or be angry—that's not what a good Christian does. But in my heart, I screamed one thing: "God, I didn't do *nothing* to you, bro! Why is this happening!"

My tanking life didn't stop there.

Over the past year, I had gotten involved in some business ventures with some guys I knew from my time in the NFL. I brought the money, they brought opportunity. Or so I thought.

After investing a year's worth of time and a significant portion of my NFL earnings with these people I used to consider friends, they used a hidden clause on a contract to rob me blind and run off with most of what I'd put in.

Now finances were added to the list of things life seemed to be taking away, and I finally gave up.

One summer night, I found my way to a liquor store. I didn't know what I was doing or why I was there, just that I needed somewhere to go. I'd never seriously drank before, but I'd heard of other people doing it when they were in tough spots. Maybe it would help. Not much, just a little bit.

I bought a pint of Jack Daniels.

The next night, I bought a liter.

And the next night, another liter.

Before long I was draining a half to full bottle every night. It didn't do anything to actually help my pain, it just numbed me to it, which in some ways was worse. The more I drank, the farther away my wife and daughter's memories felt and the more distant I was from Tyson, Tinsley, and others important in my life. Most nights, I fell asleep scared and lost, my vision clouded in a haze, my pain suppressed by liquor, and my soul no more at peace than when I started.

Then, as I drank one night, I picked up something else: a Bible.

I hadn't seriously read scripture in years. My discipline to it kind of trailed off following Ashley's death. But now, as I flipped through the old pages, I found my heart comforted.

With a half empty bottle of whiskey Jack in my hand and a black leather Bible on the kitchen table in front of me, I opened to the book of Job. I'd read his story before, but for the condition I was in, it might as well have been for the first time. Out of all the passages I could have read, Job, understandably, was the one I was drawn to.

Job was a wealthy landowner who is believed to have lived in pre-Mosaic days, perhaps anywhere from 2300 to 1500 BC in the Middle East. He followed God and God blessed him immensely with a wife, seven sons and three daughters, tens of thousands of livestock, and multitudes of servants.

In the scriptures, Job's real story begins when God starts bragging on him to Satan. Satan suggests that the only reason Job is relentlessly faithful to God is because God blesses him. *"Does Job fear God for no reason? Have you not put a hedge around him and his house and all that he has, on every side? You have blessed the work of his hands, and his possessions have increased in the* land. But stretch out your hand and touch all that he has, and he will curse you to your face." (Job 1:9-11)

In response, God makes a wager: Satan can take whatever he wants from Job short of actually harming Job's body. Essentially, "Do whatever you can to make him turn from me, and we'll see who is right."

We don't know how long after, but there came a day that started just like any other. Job was managing his business affairs, seeing to his investments, whatever. And on that ordinary day, a messenger came to Job drenched in sweat and out of breath.

"Master! The oxen were plowing and the donkeys feeding beside them, and the Sabeans fell upon them and took them and struck down the servants with the edge of the sword, and I alone have escaped to tell you." Dang, Job. That's hard.

While he was still talking, another servant fell to the floor behind the first with additional news.

"Master, the fire of God fell from heaven and burned up the sheep and the servants and consumed them, and I alone have escaped to tell you." Wow. That sucks, Job.

And while the second servant was talking, still another servant came behind him.

"The Chaldeans formed three groups and made a raid on the camels and took them and struck down the servants with the edge of the sword, and I alone have escaped to tell you." Whoa, what? Again?

And then a fourth came with the worst news of all.

"Your sons and daughters were eating and drinking wine in their oldest brother's house, and behold, a great wind came across the wilderness and struck the four corners of the house, and it fell upon the young people, and they are dead, and I alone have escaped to tell you." Man, Job. I'm so sorry.

In anguish, Job tore his robe and shaved his head, which was culturally traditional for mourning. And then, he fell on the ground and worshipped God, saying, "Naked I came from my mother's womb, and naked shall I return. The Lord gave, and the Lord has taken away."

As I read Job's story, I saw my own. I'd been financially blessed and successful, I'd been a good father and husband, I'd tithed and given freely to causes, I'd honored God on and off the field. And still, God let death and destruction come to my doorstep.

In chapter two in the book of Job, God brags on Job again to Satan, saying, "Consider my servant Job, who still holds fast his integrity!"

Satan isn't impressed.

"Skin for skin! All that a man has he will give for his life. If you stretch out your hand and touch his bone and his flesh, he will curse you to your face." And the Lord said to Satan, "Behold, he is in your hand; only spare his life." (Job 2:4-6)

Now, with full reign, Satan attacks Job's body.

"So Satan went out from the presence of the Lord and struck Job with loathsome sores from the sole of his foot to the crown of his head. And he took a piece of broken pottery with which to scrape himself while he sat in the ashes. Then his wife said to him, "Do you still hold fast your integrity? Curse God and die." But he said to her, 'You speak as one of the foolish women would speak. Shall we receive good from God, and shall we not receive evil?' In all this Job did not sin with his lips."

I read those last words, "Job did not sin with lips," and sat still for a long time.

I could see Job in my head, covered in boils from head to foot, trying to scrape the disease from his body with the sharp edge of a busted clay pot, seated in a bed of ashes to absorb the oozing liquid from his body, and shivering not from the cold but from pain. His wealth and livelihood are gone, his children are dead, and his wife despises him. He has nothing left.

Worse than my situation, but still, I could understand.

I drank Jack and rolled those words around in my head. "… not with his lips." Then, I realized that was me, too. I couldn't help but laugh.

I'd been doing all the things with my lips that Job did with his. "Hallelujah! Praise the Lord in the highest!" But in my heart, I was singing God a terrible song. I would never say it out loud or write the words, but I was singing a song about him—to him. Like Job, I always sat on the claim, "Man, I didn't say it with my mouth though! Yeah, I never sang it with my mouth, Lord!"

"Not with my lips," I thought. "I've never cursed you with my lips because… I always have to be perfect. But in my heart? No, I'm not so perfect there."

Over the next few nights, I continued to drink Jack and read Job.

Three friends of Job heard word of what happened and traveled to visit him. And when they saw him, he was so deformed and in such disarray that they didn't recognize him. And they sat on the ground with him for seven days and seven nights, and no one spoke a word.

Finally, Job spoke and thoroughly cursed the very day he was born. His friends sympathized with him before trying to offer some understanding on why this was happening. Maybe Job disobeyed God? Maybe he had slandered God? Maybe God was punishing him for something?

Job's answer was the same as so many of ours: if he's punishing me, I have no idea what for.

Still, his friends continued to lay it on him. Job defends himself. His friends press harder. "Surely you must have done something wrong for God to do this to you." Job defends himself again. "I've been righteous and uncompromising! I have a right to question God right now!" Their debate continues and continues, until finally, Job essentially cries out, "Why, God?!"

I didn't *really* understand before when I would hear Job's story in church—when I had the perfect cookie cutter life, when I had it all planned out, when it was easy to say, "I'm doing this for God! We're just a really blessed family!"

But now I understand. I understood now that the question I was forced to answer wasn't, "Do you love God?" but, "Do you *still* love God?"

In the story of Job, a fourth person then comes on the scene. Not one of Job's close friends, but a young man who came later. His name was Elihu. Finally, after listening at length to the conversation, he couldn't stay quiet any longer and entered the conversation.

"I am young in years, and you are aged; therefore I was timid and afraid to declare my opinion to you. I said, 'Let days speak, and many years teach wisdom.' But it is the spirit in man, the breath of the Almighty, that makes him understand. It is not the old who are wise, nor the aged who understand what is right. Therefore I say, 'Listen to me; let me also declare my opinion.'" (Job 32:6-10)

He then proceeds to tell Job's three friends just how askew they are in their judgment for condemning Job without finding any fault in him. And then, he turns to Job.

You think you're perfect? Think again.

You think God is in the wrong? He's not.

You wonder why God isn't answering you? Maybe because you're demanding he explain himself rather than asking for understanding. God doesn't answer arrogance.

Did you forget God's goodness and greatness? Let me remind you.

After Elihu finishes, God finally answers. But not in the way Job expected.

We know from the benefit of context that God was betting on Job in a contest with the Devil. God wasn't punishing Job, he was trusting him. It wasn't God who persecuted Job, it was Satan. But God doesn't tell Job that. He doesn't tell him why it all happened. He doesn't explain any of it.

Instead of explaining why, God reminds Job who God is.

"Where were you when I laid the foundation of the earth? Who marked its dimensions? Surely you know! On what was its foundation set? Who laid its cornerstone?

"Or who shut in the sea with doors when it burst out from the womb? Have you commanded the morning since your days began? Are you familiar with the depths of the sea? Have you seen the gates of death? Have you comprehended the expanse of the earth? Tell me, Job, if you know!

"Where does light dwell and where does darkness congregate? You know, don't you? You were born before I separated the light from the darkness and have lived so long! Right, Job?

"Can you lead forth the constellations of stars in their season? Can you send out bolts of lightning or give the power of wisdom to the mind? Do you give the horse his might or is it by your understanding that the hawk soars in the sky or can you play with Leviathan in the sea?"

In response, Job surrenders, acknowledging God's power and prevailing purpose and admitting he spoke of what he doesn't understand.

He was never told why, but he trusted the one who did know why.

And then, he recognizes the greatest gift any of us can receive: "I had heard of you by the hearing of the ear, but now my eyes see you." (Job 42:5)

No longer did Job believe in God—he *knew* God.

Rescue

My life was not so different from Job's before the storm hit.

Job prided himself on his knowledge of God, thorough righteousness, and subsequent blessings he received that boasted to the world "God is fond of me."

I was like him.

I had it all, and I thought I deserved it because of how good a person I was. I thought I had a formula worked out with God for success and salvation, and I was so caught up in how I performed for God to continue earning all my blessings that I missed the most important thing of all: having a relationship with him.

What's the difference between religion and relationship? Religion is performing for God because you want what he can give you, relationship is walking with God because you want to be close to him.

Trials have a way of tearing down your religious self righteousness. Job knows a little something about that.

Job was a good husband, father, and person. He knew of God by the tradition passed down by his forefathers. He had all his theology and behavior straight and was prideful in his abundant wealth and obvious favor with God. He knew as much about God as anyone could.

But he didn't know God personally and intimately. Not really.

Not until after the storm did he admit, "I had heard of you by the hearing of the ear, but now my eyes see you." (Job 42:5)

But to be rescued, we have to be weak.

I'm reminded of the story of a lifeguard.

There was a big-time businessman who flew home from work in New York City. He was only back for a day, and so his son asked him, "Hey, Dad, you got the day off, you wanna go to the pool?"

The father hadn't spent much time with his son lately, but he was free that day and decided it was as good a day as any to do a little something with him. "Okay, come on!" he said. They threw swim trunks on and drove a mile to the local swimming pool.

"I'll be over on the side reading the paper," the father said. "You let me know if you need anything."

As the father was reading the paper, he heard frantic cries coming from the swimming pool. Everyone was screaming. He dropped his paper and looked up to see his son flailing in the deep end of the pool trying to catch a breath.

The father was about to jump into the pool but just as he reached the edge, the lifeguard grabbed him from behind and held on to him. The father started fighting to free himself.

"Man, get off me!"

"Sir, wait!" the lifeguard said.

"Are you crazy right now? My son is drowning! Don't you see him!"

The lifeguard continued to hold. "I said wait!"

The father continued to fight. "Man, let go of me!" But he could not shake the lifeguard's embrace.

"Wait," the lifeguard said once again.

The father watched desperately as his son finally stopped flailing and the last air bubble popped on the surface. And then, the lifeguard let go.

"Clear the edge of the pool!" the lifeguard yelled, throwing the father to the side and jumping into the water. He grabbed the son, pulled him out, popped his chest one time, and the boy spit out the water, coughing and gasping for breath.

"You alright?" the lifeguard asked.

"Yes, Sir," the son said when he had caught his breath.

But the father was still so mad that the lifeguard grabbed him.

"What's wrong with you!" the father yelled at the lifeguard, "I was trying to save him!"

The lifeguard turned to the father and said, "Sir, let me tell you. In my practice, when a person is drowning, I'm trained that I cannot go into the water when they are at their strongest. If I do, they are so panicked that they expose the risk of killing us both. So I have to wait until that person is at their weakest."

That's what God does with us.

We pump ourselves up with our own strength and tell ourselves, "I'm gonna make it happen, I'm gonna pull it off, I'm doing this for God." And in our self-generated power, we turn away from the work of the Holy Spirit in us, dismiss the word of God in our arrogance, and neglect prayer as we rush forward on our own.

Then, we end up lost.

That's why I love how God says he will leave the ninety-nine sheep to find the one who is lost. And when he has found the lost sheep he will hold it in his arms against his heart. (Isaiah 40:11) Why does he hold it against his heart? So that the sheep will know it is close to the shepherd, and because it is close, it will know it is safe.

But before the sheep was found, it was lost.

Alone.

Afraid.

Broken.

Weak.

And it's in our weakness that Jesus dives in after us.

As long as we're charging on in our own strength, he'll let us. He will let seasons of weakness overtake us and let us exhaust ourselves trying to do it on our own until there is nothing left, because only in our weakness can we be rescued.

I love what Jesus tells the Apostle Paul in 2 Corinthians 12:9: "My power is made perfect in weakness."

What is weakness? Something is not going your way, something you don't understand, something is broken in your life. And God says that in that place, his strength is made perfect!

Like the lifeguard, God will let us hit rock bottom not because he has turned away, but because he is rescuing us.

Chapter 8
MORALS VS. MORALE

Cleats On

In life, just as in football, situations will rise and fall. Things will go our way and then backfire, circumstances will change on a dime, the stadium will roar for us and then against us and then make no sound at all. But we don't have to change with it. That's the power of choosing your mindset: the state of the stadium will change, but you can stay the same.

To endure is to decide who you will be and what you will do simply because it's *who you are,* not because that's how we feel or what the morale of the stadium is telling us. If we live according to the morale of the stadium we play in, we will inevitably fall with it.

That's a lesson I learned the hard way.

It was the Arizona Cardinals vs. the Chicago Bears, November 8, 2009. The day was hot, the Cardinals just regained the ball and were on first down, and I was seeing red. I'd had three quarterback sacks on the Cardinals last drive, and I was ready for another.

"Hut!"

The play exploded to life, I moved to break through the offensive line for the tackle, and then—*BOOM!* My body crashed to the ground like a tree under an avalanche. I coughed and tried to regain my breath, looking around for the freight train that just hit me. Standing over me was Deuce Lutui, a 6'4" 340-pound guard for the Cardinals who was supposed to be on the other side of the field.

The Cardinals advanced a few yards before getting stopped and I growled as I regained my feet. Shaking off the hit, I planted my feet back on the line.

The second down play ignited and I started rushing the quarterback on the right side of the ball. I saw an opening and went for it, but just as I did, I felt my legs collapse as someone tripped me. I tumbled sideways and crashed to the ground, wind knocked out of me, and saw my assailant: Deuce Lutui, again.

This time, my knee hurt when I stood back up, recalling lingering damage from my hamstring injury three years ago. I stomped my leg on the ground in defiance of the pain and gritted my teeth.

Third down, Lutui blindsided me again. I was so confused. He was starting the play positioned on the left side of the ball and I was on the right side, which meant he should have been focused on dealing with his assignment on the left side of the field. Instead, he was leaving his responsibility to come over to my side of the field and blindside me.

Fourth down was a repeat of the three previous, except this time, blindsiding me wasn't enough for Lutui. With the refs preoccupied on the ball, Lutui slammed his knee into the left side of my ribcage. To anyone watching it would have just looked like part of the tackle, but I knew better. My knee hurt, my rib cage dented. Now I was pissed off.

I jumped back to my feet and locked eyes with Lutui, glaring.

"Next time you touch me, you gon feel me," He brought that side out of me. Lutui gave me his back and strode off.

Having reached first down again, the Cardinals lined up for their next play. I planted my feet, ready to take on the line in front of me. The center snapped the ball, the play sprung to life, and as I started to rush the quarterback, Deuce Lutui blindsided me—again.

And so begins the number one search that pops up on the internet when you type in my name that I wish I could delete.

I finally lost it.

I rolled to get Lutui off of me, got my knees under myself, pinned Lutui on his chest, and then, with every drop of frustration I had, BAM! I punched him in the face mask hard enough to make his head snap back.

Lutui grabbed his face in his hands and the ref threw his flag. I glared at Lutui and yelled in my head, "I warned you, and I keep my promises!"

I don't know if "fastest ejection in NFL history" is a record you necessarily want to have, but I have it, regardless.

As I stormed off the field that day, I unwittingly cost myself a $6.5 million dollar bonus that required 74% playing time. I was cutting it close already, and getting ejected in the first minute of a game finished me off. Let alone the $5,000 fine I had to pay. In all, I learned a lesson: never let the morale change your morals.

Every day you wake up, you get to make a decision: What do I stand for? Your morals. That's what I call the Cor Uma mindset. In Latin, Cor Uma means "to live from your core." Too often, we live according to the morale of the stadium instead of from the morals of our heart. But all it takes to change that is one decision: What will your morals say about you?

The "morale" of a football game can change quickly. Morale is the confidence, enthusiasm or discipline of a group at a particular time. We may be up seven points at the beginning of a quarter and then down fourteen by the middle of the quarter. Our team starts losing confidence, our fans start losing their energy, our players start giving up because the score feels too high to come back. The opposing team seizes the momentum and the commentators say, "The morale has changed! The energy has shifted!"

Morals relate instead to who you choose to be. They're the things you stand for and won't move from. You can't control morale, but you can control your morals.

That football game with Deuce Lutui wasn't the only time I let exterior morale affect my interior morals: there are more football games than I can count, more arguments than I can count, more business ventures than I can count. When I lost my wife and my life started to crumble, I began to let my morals fall into question, and when your morals start shifting that's when your moral compass starts drifting. You begin to wander into foreign places because you no longer know what's guiding you.

But it doesn't have to be that way.

When you find yourself somewhere you never thought you'd be, remember who you are and remember what you stand for. When we're off a little, we need to get our moral compass back. Time to start adjusting and regaining our own morale. Exterior circumstances don't have to change the morale *inside of* you.

What do you stand for? Write these things down. In the morning remind yourself, "What do I stand for? Me? Today?" And choose to commit yourself to those four or five things.

For me, I decided I want big PECKS. Patience. Empathy. Compassion. Kindness. Servant. P.E.C.K.S.! If I ever forget who I am and I find myself somewhere I never would have chosen to be, I have to remind myself, I chose to have big PECKS!

When I've taught my son three times already how to wash the dishes and he forgets to use soap *again,* I choose to be patient.

When someone tells me of losing their loved one or that they're going through a divorce, I choose to have empathy.

When a single mother needs help buying groceries, I choose to have compassion.

When someone has wronged me and it's in my right to be cold toward them, I fight hard to choose kindness.

When others around me are fighting to be first and get what they want, I choose to be a servant.

What are those things for you that make up the moral compass of who you are? Those things that will deny your morale in the moments of doubt? Your morale is like weather. It's going rain, storm, sleet, snow—it's going to do all these things outside of you, but your morals are your foundation, your house, the thing that's built inside of all the exterior emotion. No matter what storm comes against your house, your morals are what keeps you.

Decide who you will be, write it down, and remind yourself daily. In time, it won't be words on paper—it be who you are.

In the months after my wife died, I found myself walking through the mall one day and noticed it was uncomfortably cold.

On a whim, I thought, "I wonder if I can change the thermostat."

I walked to the wall and looked around for the little box just to, you know, see if I could change the temperature. Curiosity had me more than anything by now. I found it, tried to open it, and low and behold, it was covered with a locked plastic case.

Normally, I would have thought nothing of it, but I was emotionally raw after Ashley's passing and losing the most important person in the world to me. I was in a place in life where I could feel everything, songs made sense, pictures were deeper than they were. Everything had poetry and motion.

I rocked back and contemplated the thermostat. "Whoa," I thought, as the thermostat spoke meaning to me.

As we are housed in this body, it is our job to put a cover over our thermostat. We do not allow anyone to come into our life and touch our settings. We already decided what they will be!

When you wake up in the morning you have the power to set who you will be today and then lock it. Don't let anyone touch your thermostat! When you get up in the morning you decide the temperature you would like to be that day, and you set it and lock your thermostat. Don't let anyone just walk up and touch it. They can admire it, they can see it, but they cannot move you up or down. Only you get to do that.

How many times in life have we allowed people to come in and change our settings? We say, "They make me angry," or, "They make me feel like I'm not loved," or, "They pushed my buttons." No! It is your job to lock your cover. What is your mindset? What do you say you will be today? What do you stand for? You have to set it. It's your thermostat, and your temperature is your own responsibility. No one else can touch it unless you let them.

So who are you and what do you stand for? You decide! No one else makes that decision for you. Not the pace of the game, not the energy of the fans, not how many points you're up or down, not how your team is performing and not the condition of the competition. Only you! No matter what is going on around you, you get to decide: who will I be today?

Get Your Power Back

The business ventures gone-bad that I got into in 2014 taught me a big lesson.

Some friends of mine from the NFL were involved in several upstart companies looking for investors. I had just finished getting my MBA and was excited to continue becoming a God-treprenuer and stepping in with these opportunities seemed perfect. They were experienced, well-seasoned professionals who I thought knew more about the business world than I did.

I jumped in. Money, contacts, influence, all of it.

Six months later, they snagged me and several other investors on a clause in the contract and robbed us blind.

At first, all I wanted to do was get my money back, but once I knew there was no way that was going to happen short of spending millions of dollars to sue them, I had to learn to let go.

Anger and spite lock you in to downward-spiraling thoughts and anti-productive patterns, sucking the life out of you and stealing all the mental energy and power you could be putting toward other things.

My damaged pride demanded I keep blaming these guys for what they did to me and justify my anger—I *deserve* to feel this way!—but the voice of truth in my heart told me otherwise. Instead, I had to learn to own up to my own choices. I refused to let these men continue to have power over me. I chose to trust people blindly that I shouldn't have, and now, I was letting them control my thermostat. Did I want them to continue to have power over me, or did I want to take my power back?

I decided to take command of my thermostat, and from that day forward I committed to myself I would never allow someone or give someone else the power to control what I did with my mental capacity, energy, and focus. I stopped blaming others, and I locked my thermostat.

You have to forgive to get your power back.

With God, you have all the power you could ever need inside of you, but not if you let someone else steal it. If you want your power back, let go. Lock your thermostat, and choose to forgive.

It's crazy how much family can bring you back down to earth. Tyson, Tinsley, and I would go to spend Christmas with our family. After months of living it up at celebrity events and sitting in big time business meetings and meeting important people, my ego would start to get inflated. Then, we'd walk into Momma's house to be with the family and everyone just knows me as TJ, the name I've had since childhood. And everyone's making jokes and jabbing around and having discussions about current events and my opinion doesn't matter more than anyone else's anymore.

But first, I remember to lock my thermostat.

Before I walk in Momma's door at family gatherings or before I have to go back into old environments, I decide who I'm going to be and lock my thermostat down. If that means I get to have extra patience, then what a gift. If that means working on my empathy, I needed the training. If that means working on my compassion, my kindness, or my servant-heartedness, then so be it, I get to become a better man because of it.

The fact is, each of us is accountable for our own actions. It doesn't matter what somebody else did to us, what they said to us, or how they treated us. We are still accountable and responsible for ourselves, and that is a good thing. Making up excuses as to why its other people's fault can feel good for a moment, but making up your mind to take command of your own life and emotions is far more rewarding. When you choose to forgive, you reclaim your own power.

This is a mechanism for how to endure. This is your life. There are a lot of people who don't mind letting others determine their worth, or judge how good they are or what they should be doing or how they need to live, but this is your life, not someone else's. You don't need someone else's permission to try something, to put your heart and back into something, to go somewhere, to grow, to change. If I'd left my life to the words of the people who did not believe in me, I would not be anywhere. If I left my life up to their standards of me I'd be in jail, no good at football, a worthless father, fat, dumb, think I was ugly, and hate myself.

No one knows what God has told you. That's yours. Don't get angry when people don't believe in you. Stand your ground, and don't let them turn you aside from your goals to hate them instead. They don't get to touch your thermostat. God doesn't speak to all of his children the same way and so don't let someone else tell you what God thinks of what you're doing. And if along the way, they try to hurt you or do hurt you, there is only one thing to do: forgive.

Forgive.

Forgive.

Forgive.

Not just them, but also forgive yourself. Jesus died on the cross for whatever you hold against yourself. He will always be the hero in your story.

Let go of anger, and take hold of your power.

Forgive, and take your power back.

Chapter 9
COUNTERFEIT
Cleats Off

I'd heard about the Hoffman Process healing retreat from a few friends over the years. It's all about getting in your head and identifying negative thought patterns in your life. They said it was life changing. For me? I am not quite there yet.

Like Job, I was stuck in my self righteousness.

God was starting to send "Elihus" into my life—people like the young man in Job's story who called him out and prepared the way for God to speak.

Vince Parker.

Joe Hall.

Anthony Adams.

My sister, Tamara.

Pastor Rob.

These were the people I poured into in my season of harvest when they most needed it; I did what I could to sow into them and build them up. And then, when I was so broken in my desolate place, all these men and women popped back up in my life to remind me of what I once told them.

Just like God sent Elihu to speak into Job, he was sending people to speak into me. They were the people I least expected, and it was becoming the craziest piece of art.

Then came the Elihu I least expected of all.

It was my seventh day at the Healing retreat in Petaluma, California. I was in a class of eighteen other people. We'd done some interesting exercises and I'd gained some new perspectives, but it was a far cry short of life changing. Plus, I had to tolerate the most annoying staff member in the world, Michael.

Michael worked for the Healing Institute as a class instructor and talked like a stuck up prick. He was this little skinny dude who talked like he owned the world. He smoked cigarettes all week and never shut up. His trademark comments, "Buh da buh" "mmm huh hmmm" constantly flew from his fast-talking mouth. He had this whole rich European vibe going with the skinny jeans and Spanish shoes and tight jacket—in my mind, all that equaled the most annoying guy ever. And this guy would not leave me alone! He didn't care about playing football or athletics or anything I liked.

Michael and I spent our days starring at each other. He'd say something and I'd just think, "Man, this guy." He corrected everybody constantly. Why did he think he was so perfect? I had it out for him.

It wasn't until later in the week that I learned the method to their madness. Each person in the process was playing a role. They were agitating you on purpose because their goal was to pull everything out of you. But I didn't know that yet.

Everyone had broken down at one point or another during the week, but not me. Which was how it should be. After all, I didn't have anything to break down about. They thought they were so clever with all their therapy and research. Like, "Everyone's got problems," but not me. I gave them enough rubbish to keep them off my back about it—"Yeah, yeah, your therapy works, good stuff, thanks"—but there was no way I was going to break like everyone else.

"God's got me," I kept telling them. "If God brought me here, he'll see me through. I'm good."

Didn't they get the message? I. Was. Fine.

On the second to last day, we were going through an exercise of "negative transference." They explained that negative-transference is when you take in the world's broken receptors. You and I might meet for the first time and I might be talking to you like I talk to everyone else, but it subconsciously reminds you of something you don't like. So you automatically no longer like me because my voice reminds you of your negative past and you transfer over something you've been through onto me, but it's your problem not mine. This happens everyday of our lives without us even realizing it.

You might say, "I don't like that guy. I don't know why, but there's just something about him I don't like." What you really don't like is how obnoxious he is because maybe that reminds you of a mother-in-law or past girlfriend.

They asked the group a question: "What's something that bothered you this week?"

Everybody went and I was the last guy. We all had to admit our negative transference on people from the week. Simple, right? Maybe you didn't like how someone breathed, or how they held their face, or how they held their posture, or how they were talking. You know, the little stuff that gets on your nerves that you don't get?

"Tommie!" Michael, the little fast-talking brat, piped up. "What was your negative transference?"

I looked at Michael. We were in the classroom, everybody else had admitted their negative transference, and I didn't want to. I didn't have anything to say.

"Nothing. I'm okay, God's in control."

Michael didn't let up.

"No. You're lying."

I glared at him, wishing it was culturally acceptable for me to get up and punch his teeth out. Was I okay? No. Far from it. No matter what I did, said, or believed, my heart continued to rip farther apart every new day. I felt the same I did when I tore my hamstring in the game against the Vikings and all my teammates dog piled me afterward. Every added player on top and every second that ticked by, my hamstring tore farther and farther until, finally, there was nothing left to tear.

My wife.

My career.

My daughter.

Gone.

No, I was not okay. I was hurt badly, I was suffocating, and I was disappointed at God. But I refused to admit it because getting hurt didn't line up with who I portrayed myself to be. I was Tommie Harris, the believing, unstoppable rockstar for Jesus who could do anything and who didn't need anyone. I didn't have anything to admit because I turned it all over to Jesus. I was good. In a way, I was feeling like Bishop, just the churchy way.

"Nothing," I said with a shrug. "It's all okay, God's in control. He's got it sorted."

Michael looked at me with that stupid, arrogant expression of his and words started pouring out of his mouth like snot from a runny nose.

"So, you telling me this whole week no one in this room bothered you? Nothing? No one did anything? No one said anything? No one pushed a single one of your buttons? Really? You lost your wife and daughter and career and everything and what, you're 'all good?' No one and nothing bothers you, huh?"

I worked hard to suppress my rising temper.

"Nah, man. Yeah, I lost my wife and daughter, but I love God, and I know he works all things for the good of those who love him. I just want to help others who…"

"STOP! BEING! FAKE!" Michael lurched forward out of his chair and screamed at me loud enough to make the room echo. "YOU'RE NOT *F***ING* PERFECT!"

And then, snap.

Five years of escalating pressure, and then, finally, with the words of one cigarette smoking prick, snap.

Like my hamstring under a pile of NFL football players, snap.

There it went.

Snap.

I glared through teary eyes at Michael. My chest rose and fell in rapid succession as I hyperventilated, my breaths coming in huge, exhaustive heaves.

And then, I exploded.

"YOU DON'T KNOW WHAT I'VE DONE! You think you could have done any better? You think you have a right to judge me? You think you could have done what I did? Who the hell do you think you are?!"

I lurched to the edge of my seat, muscles taut, hurling every word at Michael with all the pain and fury I had stored up for so long.

"I lost my wife and newborn daughter but I stayed a good dad through it all! You don't know any better than me! You don't know what I've gone through! You think you know me? You don't know me! You don't know anything! You think you're better than me? You think you're perfect but I'm not?! No, I'm not perfect! But I'm trying to do what I can! I'm not perfect! I'm not! *I'm not!*"

Sobs took over my body and I began to weep through broken words. Michael walked to me and grabbed me by my shoulders.

"There he is," Michael whispered. I dropped my head between my arms and cried. "This is who I've been waiting to meet. This is the real Tommie. It's hard to be who you didn't ask to be, but you're here, you're discovering. I've been watching you all week and you've been pretending. Halfway going through the drills, halfway sharing, acting like it's enough. I knew if I could yell at you, I could knock something off. I could get to you. You kept trying to be too cool, you kept trying to hide, you kept trying to slide everything off the back. You're angry down inside, you're mad, and you don't understand—it's okay, Tommie! It's okay to not be okay."

He grabbed me and pulled me so close, and I broke like a baby in his arms. Cigarette smoke and all. It didn't matter. This man got into my inner processor, the main board, and when that happened, there was no more BS, no more talking around it, no more running, no more fast talking, no more quicker-than-you thinking, no more. He got me, and I broke.

Looking back, I realize Michael wasn't annoying to me on accident. No, it was intentional. He intended to break my shell. And the number one thing that I have negative transference with is authoritarianism. Michael became my negative transference. I hate being talked to. Talked at. Talked down to. Manipulated. Played with mentally. That's why Michael was on my nerves all week When he yelled at me, that's when I finally snapped. From that moment on, I was submerged in vulnerability. It was like an egg shattered. The yolk was split. All the negative things I never could release, someone called it out of me. No longer did I have to be this badass I thought I was. Finally, I was able to give it all up.

For five years, I had held myself to the impossible standard of *being perfect*. I hated myself for not being strong enough. For not having it all together. For not getting over it. For not being okay.

That was my battle: to actually say *ouch*! To actually admit, that hurt! My whole life was training and never admitting that nothing hurt me. Since I was a kid in little league listening to coach after coach telling me, "You gotta be a MAN to play football! You gotta be a MAN out here!" LOL! I was only a little boy and had to listen to them tell me, "You out here crying like a little girl!" Once I started learning how to suppress saying ouch, I forgot how to say, "This is hurting me."

I find a lot of people, especially men, are right where I was. suffering from delayed pain. We say *ouch* five years later! And because of that, look how much pain we put others through by not being truthful about our feelings immediately. The hugs we didn't give, the tears we didn't validate, the sorrow we didn't let ourselves help carry the burden of.

By suppressing our own pain, we turn away from the pain others are feeling.

Finally, I let go in my heart and I dropped to my knees, tears flooding my eyes like Niagara Falls. I couldn't see. It was like I was driving through a rain storm and I couldn't see a thing no matter how fast my windshield wipers moved. For the first time in my life, I shattered. I cried, and then I started laughing while I was crying, snot all over my chin and cheeks. And as I rocked back and forth in Michael's arms, I chanted through sobs, "It's okay not to be okay, it's okay not to be okay, it's okay not to be okay…"

Elihu

I thought it had to be a preacher to deliver me those words. Instead, it was an annoying, skinny hotshot with a cigarette between his teeth who finally broke me and shattered my comfort zone. I was Job with all my self-righteousness and answers, and Michael was the Elihu I never saw coming.

When you're listening for God's voice, remember, he can work through anyone he wants. I was reminded of that right when COVID-19 started to hit the United States in February of 2020.

I was filling up my truck at Mickey's, a locally famous gas station in Killeen, Texas, and headed toward the convenience store for a bottle of Gatorade. Before reaching the doors, an obviously non-native Killeener approached me.

"Hey, man, hey…what the hell is wrong with these women from here?" An older man dressed like a Deacon of the AME church asked out of despair and curiosity. "I ain't from here."

"Where are you from?" I asked.

"Memphis! There's this girl I found myself playing around with on the internet. We were supposed to be hooking up so I came to see her, she got me changing her kids' diapers and cleaning her place and I spent all my money on a plane ticket and helping here with food. Man, I spent $3,000. Bruh I ain't got nothing left and I'm trying to get outta here, you know? I just need some money, man, whatever you got…" My wife gonna kill me when she finds out I'm gone."

I looked at him and laughed to myself. Before leaving my house that day, I'd prayed for an opportunity to help someone or speak into someone's life and be a blessing to them. This sure wasn't what I had in mind.

"Well, God, this isn't who I was looking for," I thought, "but I'll still help him."

"Sir, how old is the girl?" I asked.

"Man, that girl, she's twenty-three. I got my wife back at home, but I'm just out here getting it in with her, you know what I mean?" He chuckled.

I took a long look at the guy and wanted to throw up. He must have been at least sixty-five years old.

"You got a wife at home? Man, go home."

"You know, I want to go home. Yeah, I do. I just, I can't man, I flew all the way from Nashville to come here and get some with this girl and now she's just using me and I spent everything I had, like $6,000, man…"

I raised an eyebrow, curious how $3,000 turns into $6,000 so fast. The guy kept going.

"… but I'm trying to get back home, you know? I just, I need some money…"

I shook my head. This wasn't what I was here for.

"Listen, go home."

I turned and walked inside, and the guy left me saying you right, young buck, you right. Shortly after, a different man walked in behind me. I looked up.

"Man, who's truck is that out there?" he asked.

I smiled.

"That's mine."

"Whoa, I used to have one of those. I just had to sell it."

"Why?"

The guy shook his head.

"I used to be a high-end bartender around here, me and my wife before they shut everything down. We've been upside down on our payments. Guess that's why they say to avoid debt, right?" He tried to laugh it off. "Anyway. My wife and baby and I are in a little apartment center just down the street now. It's a dump, but…well, I guess you gotta be grateful for what you have."

He fell quiet for a minute, then, like he was regretful for it, said, "Do… uh… do you think you could buy me a gallon of milk? That's what we've been living off of so far. It'll keep us good until the economy picks back up."

"A gallon of milk?" I asked, perplexed.

"Yeah. We drink it cold in the morning and warm at night to give it some variety." He tried to laugh again, then trailed off. "But, it's okay man. You don't need to…"

"Nah, man!" I interrupted him. "I ain't buying you a gallon of milk—let's get you some *real* food."

The guy starred at me, confused.

"Go on. Pick out whatever you want. I'll get it for you."

He got the stuff. As he was carrying it to the cashier, he dropped it all and started crying.

"Man, I can't! This is too much! I don't know how to accept this."

I looked him in the eyes.

"Man, I done worked my butt off too hard in this life to not use what I've got to help others. You're going to take this."

I helped pick up the stuff off the floor and put it on the counter, paid for it, and put in the guy's arms. As we were walking out of the store, the guy tapped me on my shoulder.

"You know, God puts his face on whoever he chooses. Thank you for letting him use you."

God used a kid named Elihu to speak to Job, he used a cocky cigarette-smoker named Michael to break through to me, and he used me—retired-lost football player—to bless a man and his family who needed food.

What did any of us do to deserve to be used by God? Nothing. We were simply there.

In life, never dismiss what God might tell you through someone you never expected to hear it from, and never refuse to speak what he may have to say through you to someone else.

God puts his face on whoever he chooses.

Only Human

That afternoon at the healing retreat, each of us was given pillows and instructed to write down on them the negative patterns we had derived from our parents. I love and respect both my parents more than I could ever describe, but not one of us is without our faults. A few of the patterns I wrote down were, "Hide your pain," "Do it yourself," and "Weakness disappoints God."

After writing the patterns down, we were instructed to beat the pillows.

I went a little farther than that.

As others in the classroom punched and kicked their pillows, I grabbed mine with my teeth and both hands and roared. I ripped the pillow apart like a lion who finally caught the hyena that killed his cubs. As I ripped the pillow apart, forgiveness started flooding my heart. I let go of all anger and bitterness I had toward my mom and dad for what they did and all the broken patterns they taught me, because in my heart, I released the real person I'd been mad at all along: me.

Sometimes, what we think is anger toward others is really unforgiveness toward ourselves. Loving others starts with loving ourself. As Jesus tells us, "Love your neighbor as yourself." (March 12:31) But can we do that if we don't honestly love ourself? How many times do we say we love someone, but don't have anything in our storehouse to give? When we've gone through something traumatic, a lie we're often tempted to believe is that we're not worthy of living anymore. We're not worthy of joy anymore. We're not worthy of love anymore. But the truth is, to love others, we have to love ourselves and receive Christ's love first.

When we receive God's love and love ourselves, it won't make us tired to love others, because we have an abundance! No longer is it something we have to muster up—we're overflowing with it! And part of loving yourself is forgiving yourself.

We have the power of transformation in our words, and what we tell ourselves will either drive us deeper into self-hatred or lift us toward forgiveness. That's what I started to learn as I tore my pillow apart, speaking over myself over and over, "It's okay not to be okay. I'm not perfect and that's okay. I'm not strong enough and that's okay!"

Finally, only frayed strips and fluff remained of the pillow, and along with it, I shredded my self-hatred with self-forgiveness. I wasn't strong enough, I didn't have it all together, I was hurt, and that was okay! All along I was just a kid trying to be a man who had all the answers, who knew everything, who had it all under control. Finally, I didn't have to pretend anymore, and I could just be the kid.

"I don't know and I'm scared sometimes and I don't know what I'm doing, and it's okay!" I finally allowed myself to admit.

For the first time in my life, I realized that I didn't have to play God. I didn't have to be this guy who has it all figured out. I serve the one who does, I work for the one who does—I'm not the one. I was exerting myself trying to be Jesus rather than simply serving him. God sent him to die for me on the cross, not me! Without him, I'm nothing! I'm not strong enough—that's the whole point! Because he is! Jesus already did it!

In my pain, I had tried to switch roles with God where I was trying to be him. I was trying to recreate the crucifixion on myself! Persecuting myself! Crucifying myself! I couldn't even enjoy a single day cause I done messed up! I was someone trying to be Jesus! But what's the use of trying to crucify yourself when someone already did it for you and that's why you follow him? Do you believe in Jesus or not? If you do, then accept he died for you and loves you. He dies for you so you don't have to!

> *In my pain, I had tried to switch roles with God where I was trying to be him.*

This is for whoever needs to hear it: Stop trying to be God, and be his kid. God meets his children where they're at. You don't have to get it all together first.

We're only human—let God be the hero.

I wasn't strong enough, I didn't have it all together, I couldn't make it alone. Thinking that I could kept me on a rat race of trying to play a God who had already done it—sent his son who died on a cross for my sin, defeated the grave, and set the captives free. He already did it. My job wasn't to re-do it, it was to simply be his child.

I've tried everything else.

I've spent a lot of money seeking out other avenues to healing.

You can't buy your way there, you can't cry your way there, you can't beg your way there—you have to live your way there—to grow your way there. You actually gotta live.

Chapter 10
SPLITTING THE DOUBLE TEAM

Cleats On

Kenny Washington was my coach in high school. He was big, bald, and loud, and one of the few men in my life who could ever break through my barriers and touch the real me. He's the one who taught me how to fight pressure with pressure.

"Double team, Tommie!" he'd say, putting two lineman on me. "Alright Tommie, split 'em."

I'd try. I was young and strong and I'd push with everything I had to break between my two opponents, but there were two of them, and just one of me. They'd push me back a couple yards before coach Kenny would break in.

"Are you stronger than both of them?" he'd demand.

I'd shake my head.

"Think you're gonna push 'em both back?"

"No."

"Then stop trying to! Get in position again. Let me teach you something. When you feel him pressing on your right shoulder, don't push back. It's like rocking a refrigerator. Instead, take that pressure he's putting on you and use it to push back against your other opponent on your left. He's pushing on you and you're pushing on his teammate. So whatever pressure they're putting on you, you're using it against them. You fight pressure with pressure. That's how you split a double team."

In the NFL, I was a comparatively small guy for a tackle but thanks to Coach Kenny, I was the king of splitting double teams. It was my specialty. And it's a lesson that's often served me in life as well when I feel like I'm being jumped or dumped on.

Fighting pressure with pressure happens when you take whatever is pushing against you and you find something to push against. That's how you polish a diamond. You take an ugly situation and you apply its pressure to something else. You refine it. You push it into something.

In the 2006 season following my torn hamstring injury, the hits kept coming, the pressure kept building. I lost my million dollar commercial with Tiger Woods and Gatorade, not to mention my shot at winning defensive player of the year. Add to that the pure fact that my body had lost its strength.

As my conquered mounted up weekly wins on its way to the Super Bowl, I lay bedridden in Dallas with no promise of what awaited me, watching my brothers go to war without me. To save my sanity, I literally had to commit myself to every day of rehab like it was playing a football game. Every. Single. Day. I did leg raises and hip stretches 1,300 miles away. Pressure was being applied to me, and rehab was where I could send it all. I committed myself every day with the same intensity I had when I wore a jersey. This was training, and in return, I gained more and more each day. I got bigger, stronger, and faster.

This happened again when I lost Ashley. I wasn't able to control the hurt I was feeling but I was able to master my own life. I went straight into fitness. I started to refine my body, change my eating habits, and read books. I made up my mind to read four books a week. Done, finished, completed. I wanted to know how to read fast and get information quick. I trained myself there. Then I wanted to put myself in the best health position. Did that. I wanted to know how to get up, meditate on God's word, and pray. So I set a time. I couldn't do anything about what happened, but I could decide who I was going be moving forward. I took all the pain and anger and I found an outlet to put it into to and refine myself through the rehab. I had a pressure being applied to me, and I found something to put pressure on.

When we go through gut-wrenching heartache, it's tempting to just stop. Stop learning, stop growing, stop becoming more. It feels like there's no way out, so why try? Why bother trying to overcome when it feels like there's no way that you can? When it feels like your hope was stolen from you, you just keep pushing. Fighting your breakthrough is predicated on how much pressure you're willing to apply.

I know what it's like to ask those questions. Here's what we have to remember: When you're taking on a double team, something's coming free in your life—but only if you can split it! If you can split this double team, something's coming free! Fight pressure with pressure if troubles are applied in your life where do you go to disperse it? Remember, energy never dies; it only continues. I had to learn to take what was pressing me and push it into something I wanted to be better at. I wanted to finish my MBA. I wanted to be a great Father. I'm still working on that while trying to split the thought of everyday nostalgia of their mother not being here. Some days can literally feel like I'm being double teamed.

If you let doubt start taking over your mind, you'll never get anywhere. Destroy doubt. Don't think like that, don't talk to yourself like that, don't see with that perspective. We take what's meant to mean us ill, and we put all these disturbances and turbulence into something *we* command. We command what we want the result to be. But you have to commit to it: You will become better. You will come out of this situation. You have to commit to believe it, because as a man thinketh, so is he.

The Courage to Go for Breakthrough

There's an old story I heard about six Navy recruits going through training. For the recruits' final rights of passage, they had to sail through the roughest parts of the sea in a little canoe. A well-seasoned and experienced Master Chief is with them. As they're sailing, a storm overtakes them and throws the already difficult waters into turmoil.

"Row forward!" the Master Chief cried out, navigating through the turbulent water.

The recruits followed command.

"Backwards!" The Master Chief shouted again, working to keep their canoe pointed into the waves and not sideways to them.

As the violent waves beat against their canoe some of the recruits began to fear, but the Master Chief wasn't fazed. He'd been on this expedition many times and was well familiar with it.

Just as they were getting close to breaking out of the storm, they saw a humongous, wave curling ahead of them.

"We're not going to make it!" one of the recruits cried out.

The Master Chief grabbed the man with both hands.

"No, you already have!" he yelled through the spray of salt water.

"Sir?"

The Master Chief looked around the canoe and met the eyes of his frightened recruits.

"I said, you've already made it!"

As all the men grabbed hold of each other to brace for the wave, the Master Chief yelled in their ears at the top of his lungs, "See yourself on the other side of the wave!"

The recruits stared wide-eyed at the approaching wave, the canoe sailing toward it like a surfboard into a tsunami.

"You must believe it!" the Master Chief yelled. "Believe it right now—we're already on the other side! Say it with me! Tell me you see yourself on the other side of the wave!"

Just as the canoe reached the bottom of the wave, the crest finally broke and a hundred billion gallons of water came crashing down.

"Agh!" the recruits yelled their defiance even as the wave dropped. "I see myself on the other side of the—"

And once they said "wave," boom! They exploded through the other side. And as they looked around wide eyed, the Master Chief said, "Why are you surprised? We saw it already."

Have you ever felt like you're on a canoe in a storm facing a wave? I know what it feels like.

The moral of the story is to approach challenges in life with vision that sees to the other side. You have to see yourself on the other side of the wave. You have to choose to *see* hope.

The Bible tells us in Hebrews 11:1, "Now faith is the assurance of things hoped for, the conviction of things not seen." Without hope, we have nothing to act on. Nothing to endure for. Nothing to point our faith toward. It is hope that allows us to play in the marketplace of possibilities of what God can do.

You cannot endure without hope. That is one of the main ingredients of endurance. You have to choose to see it! I know it's ugly, I know it's so uncomfortable, I know it's terrifying, but seeing to the other side of the wave is how you find the courage to stay the course! is how you breakthrough!

You must see it to make it, and you must speak it to see it. Say it with me: "I still believe God said he will never leave me nor forsake me! Even here!"

What you say impacts what you believe! So say it with me again: "I still believe God's promises!"

When you feel alone and afraid, say it again: "God, you said you will never leave me, and I'm holding on."

It doesn't matter what situation comes. Good or bad, victorious or desolate. When you throw your fists in the air and know you're still the heavyweight champion of the world, say it: "And still God, I believe." When it's your daughter who dies without cause, "And still God, I'm holding on." When it's your friend who falls, "And still God." When it's your mother or father, "And still."

The overcomers are those who choose to believe on a daily basis that, "Yes, I'm going through what I'm going through, I'm fighting through what I'm fighting through, but it won't be like this always!"

Breakthrough is the mindset to see yourself on the other side of the wave. Yeah, the wave is crashing. Yeah, it looks big. But you have to choose the belief system that says, "I'm already on the other side!"

Going for the breakthrough is as hard to mentally decide as it is to actually do.

Waves are big and double teams aren't fair.

When we face gut-wrenching heartache, it's tempting to just stop. Stop learning, stop growing, stop becoming more. But living requires growing. We can't just stop. We can't give up. I know it feels hopeless when a wave is crashing over you or you've got a double team on you, but don't give up. Choose to believe, and don't be swayed by the voices of others.

The voices will say it's hopeless.

The voices will say it's your fault.

The voices will say God left you.

Don't listen to them.

We are in the potter's hands. At sixteen we're one way. At twenty-one, another. At thirty-three, still another. We're in the potter's hands, and if people don't like what they see, tell them, "I'm being molded." Tell them, "God has me under construction. Be patient with me. God is not through with me yet. I am still running my race." Know this truth: God created you to do great things, and if this terrifying wave is part of your great thing, so be it. It's painful, but it's necessary.

It's like training camp. No one likes training camp during the week but everyone likes playing on Sundays. Everyone hates two-a-days, training camp, but that's where all the work is developed. That's where the wheat and the weeds are sorted. That's the separation process. Who talks about it and who's about it. God is preparing us for the Sundays in our life, and he's sorting his players by whoever makes it through these three weeks of camp. The Sundays are those days when God sets the proper crowd around us and we're able to tell the goodness of God, and we're prepared for it because we've trained through hard situations.

Don't give up. I know double teams are hard and waves are scary, but they can be broken.

Fight pressure with pressure, and you can split the double team.

See the other side, and you will break through the wave.

Chapter 11
ENOUGH!
Cleats Off

In October of 2018, in Frisco, Texas I stood in the Dr. Pepper Stadium locker room shower. It was Red River weekend and I had just finished playing in the celebrity softball tournament. After waiting an hour for a clear shower, I was finally able to work on washing the sweat and dirt from my arms.

The Red River Shootout is an annual rivalry game between the Oklahoma Sooners and Texas Longhorns, and prior to the big game are always a number of smaller games and events that take place over the weekend. One of those events in particular is the Red River Celebrity Softball Tournament, in which celebrities are intermingled into teams with wounded military veterans. The team coaches this year were Matthew McConaughey with the Longhorns and country singer Toby Keith with the Sooners.

Half of Toby's team were military veterans, while the other half was made up of other country singers, baseball players, and football players. Toby was a longtime OU fan and had been friends since way back when I played for the Sooners., He brought me onto his team as one of his recruits. Running bases and swinging a bat were a little different than the sport I was used to, but a true athlete will be an athlete!

As I showered in the locker room, I started hitting a little tune. I don't know what it is about hot water and getting clean that makes it such a perfect time for singing, but it just is. An impromptu melody popped into my head and I hummed it up and down.

"Who sang that?" someone yelled several showers down. It sounded like Billy Dawson, one of the country singers on our team. I became friends with him a year prior at the same event.

"Tommie!" I answered from the shower stall.

"Sing that again, brother!"

I hit it again.

"Man! You sound like a little mix of Chris Stapleton and Ray Charles!"

"Man, get out of here, don't try to gas me, Billy!" I called back.

"No, for real! I know what I'm talking about. You got a little country in there, a little gospel! You ever done an album?"

"Nah. I played around a little while in the pros but haven't thought about it since then. Wasn't ever serious about it."

"You need to get down to Nashville and we can put you up!"

I laughed.

"Man, you're playin'."

I'd had it happen more than once where some guy started hyping me up and grabbed my number and never followed through, and I wasn't wasting my time anymore.

"You forget who you talkin' to Tommie? It's Billy D.! I'm serious! Get your butt down to Nashville!"

I ended up reconnecting with Billy before we split ways. Maybe he was the real deal, maybe he wasn't, but I decided to call his bluff.

I'm glad I did. Next thing I knew, I was landing in Nashville and Billy was picking me up.

That first day, we made a stop at the Nashville Penitentiary where Billy works with the Redemption Songs program to help inmates write their own story into music. Each inmate works with a different song writer and over the course of a few weeks they get to create their own song. They can rap, sing, whatever they want to do. The main goal is to simply stimulate their creative process and help them release pain in their life through music. It was in that penitentiary, watching Billy and the other song writers work with the inmates at steel tables, that I started to learn what it took to write songs.

After a while, Billy came over and dropped into a seat next to me.

"So what do you think?"

I looked around the room and took it all in again.

Feeling like I was in the Blues Brothers scene in jail as each inmate took their time being coached with a pro then had a turn to perform. It was an amazing "jail-house rock" kind of moment with inmates singing and jamming.

"This is how songwriting works?" I said with a smile.

"Pretty much! Tell the story, chop it into lyrics, harmonize it to a melody. Some of these guys aren't the greatest singers, but the process is still valuable. Music helps you bring meaning to the things you were never able to talk about before." Everything sounds better through music.

"That's the truth."

Billy swung one leg over the other and leaned back.

"How did you learn to sing?"

I shrugged.

"I don't know if I ever really learned. My dad loved singing and I just picked it up from him as a kid. We still go off when we're together!"

Billy laughed.

"It's good for the soul."

"It is."

"So you're decided on country?"

" No. Soul Country," I countered.

"Yeah. I like that country lets you focus more on the story than on getting lost in the beats and sounds. It just fits my story better."

"I agree. Bet I get some heat though," I said, laughing. "Not a lot of black guys in the country space. My friends say I should do hip hop or R&B. Just too cliche for me."

Billy laughed, too.

"Find whatever lets you share your story the best. That's the whole point. You've written some of your own stuff before, right?"

"Just messing around. Some poems. Some worship pieces. Some words to my wife. Not much."

"What was she like?"

"Man. She was the most kind, gentle, humble woman you ever met. She knew how to love people right where they were. When she passed away, I never saw it coming."

"How did you feel when you were going through everything?"

I stared at the concrete wall for a moment, thinking and remembering all the pieces of my journey.

"Deflated, bro. Totally deflated."

Billy leaned forward.

"That's it. You need to write that down. Deflated."

He tossed me a spiral notebook and a pen. I scribbled the word "Deflated" on the top of a page.

"Jason!" Billy called to another songwriter across the room. A man with long, graying hair looked up. "Come over here!"

"This is Jason Matthews," Billy said to me, introducing us. Then to Jason, "Tommie's a friend of mine from Dallas with a deep story. Think you can help me pull it out of him?"

We spent the next thirty to forty-five minutes bantering and writing things down. I never would have guessed that a penitentiary would be the place to write my first song, but with some of the most talented Nashville writers and artists gathered there, I couldn't have gone anywhere better.

"Try, 'I was deflated,' with a melody," Billy told me.

I let my feelings take over and sang what came to me.

"Love it!" Billy said. "Give me some more melody."

We didn't have the words yet, but we started imagining the sound anyway, coming up with the words and melody at the same time. "Hmm, hmm, hmm, that's what I've said! Hmm, hmm, hmm, I love you! Hmm, hmm, that's what!"

"Okay. Now, where were you?"

"The airport."

"What time was it?"
"About 8:45."
"Where else were you?"
"I landed, went to baggage claim, and that's when I got the call."
"Airport… baggage claim… Claim… Plane rhymes with claim. Airplane and baggage claim. That works."

And that's how we rolled. In no time at all, we had the intro and first verse down:

> At 8:45 I was flying high on an airplane
> Then I got a call that changed it all at the baggage claim
> Said she passed away and my heart just cracked
> All the money in the world couldn't bring her back
> Every breath in my chest just left, like, that

As the song started to take form, it felt like I was starting to breathe again.

A year before, some old football friends and I took a weekend getaway at a house off the river for the 2018 Super Bowl. We had a good time fishing off the dock, talking, and catching up on life, and I talked nearly non-stop about my wife. At first, I thought I was just letting the guys in on my life and learning to talk about my story, but my friend Rohan Marley noticed something I didn't.

The Philadelphia Eagles took the win over the New England Patriots, and as we were talking out by the water after the game, some of the younger guys I'd recently met started asking about Ashley. So I started telling them. I told them about how I missed her so much, about how hurt our family was, about how unfair death is, on and on even finding myself crying all over the place while explaining.

Funny how the tables flipped. A year ago, I couldn't even admit I was hurt by my wife's passing, and now, I couldn't stop talking about how bad I was hurt.

I was a few minutes into my lamentation when Rohan walked up, locked eyes with me, and shouted, "ENOUGH!"

I was pinned by his gaze and stunned, unable to look away. Rohan and I knew each other from years of being in the league. We knew similar friends and had done a lot of mission work together in Haiti, New York, and Africa. He was like a big brother to me and was one of the few people who could raise his voice at me without me punching him in the face.

"I've been listening to you sulk in your past all weekend. I love you, Tommie. I love you enough to get in your business and be straight up with you, bro. Listen to me: death is a job for the dead! Let the dead bury the dead. Living people don't worry about dead things. Death is not your responsibility. Yes, Ashley is gone. It happened. But The Most High has her. Right now, the hardest thing for you to do is to try to live. Have the courage to live! That's your only responsibility."

Enough! Death is a job for the dead. Your responsibility is to have the courage to live!

Rohan's words echoed in my head.

There wasn't a bunk bed for you in the casket, I thought.

I've learned that in order to move forward you first have to acknowledge where you are, but I'd done the first part already. I'd faced my pain. Now, it was time for me to do the second part: live.

A year later as I wrote lyrics in the Nashville penitentiary, I started to let go.

It's true that there really is healing power in music. Healing doesn't mean that your wound goes away, but it does mean that it becomes a scar. You can still see it. You can still rub your fingers over it and touch it. It is still a part of you and stands out against the skin of your story, but it doesn't hurt anymore.

With every new word I wrote of my song, another raw, open wound finished becoming a scar.

I was deflated!
Empty and naked

I had to learn to stand down on my knees
Suffocating
Didn't think I would make it
But in order for God to breath life back into me
I had to be
Deflated

Your journey to healing may not look like someone else's. It may take longer and it may be harder, and that's okay. God's timing is perfect.

Don't despise the process.

In 2018, I wasn't ready to let go of my pain, but I was ready for someone to tell me to. Thank you, Rohan.

In 2016, I wasn't ready to acknowledge I was hurt, but it was time for me to. Michael got in my grill and broke through to me.

In 2014, my daughter passed away. My business partners sabotaged me. All but a few of my friends abandoned me. And when I thought I was completely alone, God used the story of Job to help me hold on to his hand and remind me he would never leave me nor forsake me.

In 2012, when I thought I was ready to play in the NFL again, I was rejected. I didn't like it in the moment, but now, I understand it gave me the space and time I needed to be broken. If I'd had my NFL status to hide behind, it may have taken me years longer to ever learn to be vulnerable.

Ashley passed away February 12, 2012. It took me three years to talk about it publicly, seven years to admit it still hurt, and eight years to take the first step in moving forward. And I'm still learning. It doesn't have to take you that long, but I also want to encourage you, it's okay if it does.

After writing *Deflated*, I found myself scrutinizing the meaning of that word and its many applications. In the financial market, for example, when the market is down, panicked sellers scramble to get out, selling their stock at discounted rates, but it's in the deflated market that the professionals lean in. Rather than selling, they're buying, because they believe the market is going to recover. They hold on. And because they hold on, when the market finally does rebound, they emerge with profit.

What an image of hope! It doesn't matter how long it takes you or how many times you have to "let go" *again,* you can't ever give up hope.

In football, a big hit can knock the wind clean out of you and leave you completely breathless for what feels like minutes. In reality, it's only a few seconds, but as you lay gulping for air on the ground and can't get any, you think you're going to die. When you finally do catch a breath, the rush of hope that "I'm not going to die!" is as good as the breath of air itself.

But just because you caught a breath doesn't mean you can now breathe easy.

After that first breath, you might still struggle for your next breath, and then the next one, and then the one after that. The back of your throat might hurt and your lungs might scream with pain as they work to re-inflate. But never forget the truth: If you continue to fight for breath, you will run and live again.

Beauty from Ashes

I've talked to more people in broken places than I can count. A woman whose husband came home one night with another woman, loaded his things up, and left her with three kids. A kid whose parents died in a car crash and was stranded in the foster care system. A man whose home exploded in a natural gas leak that resulted in the death of his daughter.

When you've been through pain, you know how to relate to people in it.

You know that they want a hug, not advice.

You know that Bible verses sting like alcohol in a wound.

You know that nothing makes sense.

You know that sometimes you want to forget more than you want to heal.

But if I can share this with you, as someone who has been through pain and is coming out the other side: God can turn the pain you never would have chosen into the craziest, most beautiful piece of art that you never could have imagined. As God promises Israel in Isaiah 61:3: "to those who mourn in Zion—to give them a beautiful headdress instead of ashes, the oil of gladness instead of mourning, the garment of praise instead of a faint spirit; that they may be called oaks of righteousness, the planting of the Lord, that he may be glorified."

That's what writing *Deflated* was all about. It was the first step in allowing God to take my greatest pain and make something beautiful out of the ashes. And as I wrote it, I couldn't help but remember the story behind another song that was a long-time favorite of mine.

Horatio Spafford was a prominent lawyer and businessman in Chicago in the 1800s. He and his four daughters had made vacation plans in England where their friend, evangelist Dwight L. Moody, would be preaching. But due to business demands, Horatio ended up having to send his family on ahead without him. As a real estate investor, some of Horatio's properties had burned down in the Great Fire of Chicago and he was stuck dealing with the aftermath.

Several weeks later, Horatio received a letter from his wife. Like any father, I imagine he was excited for word from his family as he tore open the seal.

He had no idea what he was about to learn.

In the letter, his wife told him how the *Ville du Havre* steamboat that she and their four daughters had taken for their cross-Atlantic voyage had wrecked while at sea. Two-hundred, twenty six people had died, including their four daughters. "I alone survived. I don't know what to do. Please come quickly."

Horatio boarded the next available ship. Without the benefit of cellphones or airplanes to contact his wife immediately, he was subject to a week or more at sea. It was in that time that he wrote one of the world's greatest songs: *It Is Well With My Soul.*

He turned ashes into beauty. And that is what I was doing with *Deflated.* I used the worn-out tools of my heart and experience to create something beautiful. It's exactly what Jesus does with our faith. Faith is his tool to build beautiful things out of dark ashes we sometimes find ourselves in here on Earth.

It took years of pain for that song to come forward. I never could have written it in the middle of my pain. I wasn't able to see what God was doing then. But now, on the other side, I was able to look back and understand that, "In order for God to breathe life back into me, I had to be deflated."

What does that line mean?

Like Job, I was full of myself. Yeah, Jesus was my King, but more in concept than in truth. I lived *for* God more than I lived *with* him, and for that, I was full of self-pride. I considered all the blessings I had to be my own accomplishment. So in order for God to fill me with his breath, I first had to be deflated of myself.

A fair question then is, did God cause it?

Or like Tyson asked years ago, "Did Jesus kill mommy?"

I've wondered myself plenty of times. Did God cause the aneurysm that took my wife? The answer I've come to is *no*, I don't think so.

God desires to have relationship with creatures who rejoice in him, turn to him, find themselves in him, and love him. That requires giving humans a dangerous power: choice. The power to turn toward God or away from him. And inevitably, a world filled with choice will be a world filled with both beauty and brokenness.

That's why we live in a broken world, and that's what God's story is all about. He is working the redemption of mankind so that someday, all things will be made new with mankind's power of choice still intact. That day of wholeness is still coming and so there is still brokenness along the way, but we can also participate in the beauty right now.

We can't undo what's done, we can't justify it, we can't pay for it. But we don't live in the past, we live forward. Redeeming death is God's job. Our job is to simply live in the wake of the new thing he is doing, the new thing he is trying to teach us, the exciting relationship he is trying to build with us. Committing to the beauty God makes doesn't change the past. That's not the goal. What it does is transform our future.

I can hear many of you thinking, "But I am not a singer, Tommie." Let me assure you that music is just one avenue.

What's your gift?

Maybe for you, it's writing a book or a letter. Maybe it's painting a piece of art. Maybe it's building something out of wood or restoring an old vehicle. Whatever it is, I challenge you to find your unique way of using your gifts and story to make something beautiful.

Living doesn't mean you fix what happened. It means you trust it to God to make something beautiful out of it. You move forward.

Are you ready to live?

Let's go.

Chapter 12
OVERCOMER
Cleats On

Two minutes, forty-five seconds left in the 4th quarter. We were down 12-16 against the Minnesota Vikings at their home stadium, the Hubert Humphrey Metrodome. We had just let the Vikings score another field goal and now had just lost our possession. It was the Viking's ball again, and in such a low scoring game as this, it felt like the final nail in the casket.

As the Viking's attacked on their first and second downs, I could feel the morale of my team plummeting. No point in wasting effort on a lost cause, right?

The Vikings called a huddle, no doubt to plan a way toward what they imagined would be their next touchdown. They thought they were going to score again. They thought they were going to rub our faces in the dirt. They thought they had the momentum.

I was about to change that.

As I jogged to the sideline with my defense, I saw despair written all over coach Steve Wilks' face. It matched the expressions of the rest of the team. I understood. It was going to take a touchdown to win this and we hadn't scored one all game, just field goals. Maybe we had still had a chance several minutes ago, but now we were down to the final three minutes and had given up our possession of the ball. We had three and half minutes to make a turnover, march our way fifty yards down field, and score a touchdown that had eluded us all day.

The momentum was just going the wrong direction. Time to give up.

But not for me.

"I don't know what y'all staring at the ground like that for!" I yelled at coach Wilks and my defense. "The game ain't over 'till it's over. We just need the ball back. We get it back, and we'll win this. You listening to me? As long as there's still time on that clock we're not done here! Snap out of it. We can do this!"

The guys on the sideline stood up straight and yelled back, "Defense up!"

As we stepped back on that field, I asked myself one question: *what would you do if you weren't afraid?*

In the NFL, I never knew what to think about people praying that their team would win. What happens when a Bears' fan is praying that we win and a Vikings' fan is praying that they win? But what I was sure about was this: I had an edge because I was God's son.

In *The Lion King* movie, long after Mufasa has died and Simba has run away, there's a scene where Simba is led to a pool of water by his father's old friend Rafiki, the baboon. Rafiki tells Simba that his father is there, but when Simba arrives, he sees nothing but the pool.

"That's not my father, that's just my reflection," Simba sighs.

"No, look harder," Rafiki urges.

Simba looks again, and as he stares into the pool, he sees what Rafiki came to show him: his father's likeness in him.

"You see, he lives in you."

Just then, Simba is transported into a vision where a cloud fills the night sky and he hears a voice overhead.

"Simba…"

Simba looks up.

"Father?"

"Simba, you have forgotten me," Mufasa says in the vision.

"No! How could I?" Simba answers.

"You have forgotten who you are and so have forgotten me. Look inside yourself, Simba. You are more than what you have become. You must take your place in the circle of life."

"How can I go back? I'm not who I used to be."

"Remember who you are. You are my son, and the one true king. Remember who you are. Remember."

As the vision fades, Simba breathes deeply for the first time in years, allowing himself to be re-inflated with the power of his real identity. And then he goes and kicks butt, defeating his evil uncle who stole the throne and restores the land.

What was Simba's power? Remembering his identity.

In moments of doubt, I've learned to remember who I am. And who I am is really about *whose* I am.

What would you do if you weren't afraid?

That's where the power is! If you weren't afraid, imagine what God could do through you! The only thing getting in the way is the watered-down, fake version of you that you slip into when you're afraid.

To live in power unrestricted by fear, we have to remember who we are. Say it with me: "I am God's son or daughter. And if God is with me, I don't care who is against me!"

Fearlessness is the fruit of real identity. As the apostle Paul reminds us in Romans 8:15, "For you did not receive the spirit of slavery to fall back into fear, but you have received the Spirit of adoption as sons, by whom we cry, 'Abba! Father!'"

When we remember who we are in Christ, we have an edge in the game, because we never have to be afraid.

I stepped onto the line of scrimmage and crouched down, ready for the snap. I looked at the clock. Two minutes, forty-five seconds. The score was right next to it but I didn't care about that. In all my years playing football, I learned a secret: the scoreboard lies.

The scoreboard shows how you're performing in moments of the game. "You're down twenty eight points. You've already lost. There's no point in pushing yourself anymore. Give up." Or,

"You're ten points ahead, you can relax a little. You can take it easy now. Fifty percent effort will get the job done from here."

In every game I played, I always made up my mind ahead of time what kind of player I was going to be. Yeah, the scoreboard would fluctuate, but I never wanted my determination to change with it anymore than I wanted the scoreboard in life to dictate how I lived. All that mattered was what I did with the time I was given.

All that mattered was what I did with the time I was given.

In every game, I set my motivation on being the very best player I could be. Anything less than my absolute best was disrespectful to my team, dishonorable to God, and an insult to myself. The scoreboard in one game never changed my determination to be the best I could be. I wanted that whole offensive line, offensive coordinator, and coach I was playing against to stay wide awake in fear the full night before the game because they knew they were going to be facing me the next day.

As the Viking quarterback ran through his cadence I coiled back in my stance, cocked and ready. It was third down and the crowd was loud. Everyone counted us out. They thought we were done for. But not on my watch.

One thought dominated my mind: *We just need the ball.*

The left guard was sitting in a light stance, fingertips pressed to the ground with his butt in the air. To me, that was a clear sign he was either pulling or getting ready to pass protect. I grinned beneath my mask.

I'd been waiting to see this look the whole game.

"Set hut!" the quarterback yelled.

I jumped the count right as the ball moved and was on the left guard's trail in seconds. He moved to the right and just as he snatched the quarterback's handoff I exploded forward, colliding head-on with the running back. BOOM! I *almost* grabbed the handoff, but still, the ball was knocked loose and on the ground. It was a fumble and my defense was on it immediately, recovering the ball with a minute and fifty-three seconds left. That's what it means to count on your huddle!

The crowd went wild!

"I told you it ain't over yet!" I yelled as I ran to the sideline.

The Vikings' momentum was broken and we were on the attack now. That shifted the game. On our second down, our quarterback Rex Grossman threw a twenty-four-yard touchdown to Rashied Davis. Touchdown! 19-16! Bears for the win!

Just seconds ago the energy said to quit, but I couldn't, because I wasn't playing from the thrill of the scoreboard, I was playing from the power of who I knew I was. I was determined to be an overcomer.

Hurdles

I was watching a track meet a couple years ago, just a little while after my friend Rohan Marley got in my grill. Track and field is one of those sports you have to have competed in to appreciate. I've watched my share of meets over the years, but in this particular one, I felt like God gave me an illustration.

I love track and field because of the way the athletes train. Training a track athlete is a unique way of training compared to football. In football, everything is fast paced and anaerobic. Shut up, run, go again. In track, every athlete is told how many laps, sprints, and jumps they will have in practice so that the coaches can weigh the athletes out-put of max effort. Football is just effort, not max effort.

Thinking about it, I wonder if God may be building more runners than football players because really, life is not about hitting or being hit, it's about whether or not you gave max effort today regardless of what took place?

Watching runners race allows me to see the comparison of real life. Some people are out ahead at times, some people come out the blocks slow and some fast, but in the game of life, it's not how you start that matters, it's how you finish. Every human being's finish line is different.

But on this particular day, the event that caught my eye the most was the hurdles race where the track is filled with intentional obstacles to test the athlete's athleticism. And as I watched, I felt like God gave me a vision.

I was sitting down in front of a hurdle while sprinters were flying past me on either side. Six lanes full of people just running in open lanes. But from my view, I was sitting in a lane full of hurdles.

In my heart I asked God, "God, what is this? What does this mean?" And he said, "Tommie in your life, you've always compared your race to sprinters. 'Looks like they're going places faster and getting through things faster.' But I want you to fix your eyes straight ahead. And I want you to commit to your lane every day."

"What do you mean?" I asked.

"In order for your race to start moving forward again, you're going to have to commit daily to get over some things."

"But God, why do I got to get over some things and they're just sprinting?"

"Because they're learning to sprint right now. Don't worry about them. Right now with you, I'm building something in you that's different."

"What's that?"

"I'm building an overcomer."

If you feel like your lane has hit you with so many obstacles and you're constantly comparing your life to people who are moving and you just feel like you're not, I'd consider that just maybe I am building an overcomer. And as an overcomer, your job is to start getting over some things.

"Yeah, but my dad wasn't there when I was little," you might say. You got to get over it so your race can move.

"I was touched when I was little." You gotta get over so your race can move.

"Yeah I was cut from the team." Get over it.
"I was dropped from school." Get over it.
"I was fired and went broke." Get over it.

Why? Because it's your race. That's the only way it moves. God is building an overcomer in you! How do I know? Because if he weren't, we wouldn't be having this conversation.

You gotta start getting over some things. I don't say that in a mean way, I'm saying it because your race will stagnate until you finally go address that thing that's been holding you. And once you address it, it's time to get over it.

Let's go. We got a race to run.

It might hurt. You might limp for a while. I know I did. You might be scared of tripping over another hurdle. It might take some time for you to get your stride back, but the question isn't if you can start out perfect, the question is, are you ready to start making your way back to llving?

Like the prize race horse, make sure you put your blinders on everyday. Your life is unlike any others. It's your race, not anyone else's. As the author of the book of Hebrews compels us in Hebrews 12:1-3, "Therefore, since we are surrounded by so great a cloud of witnesses, let us also lay aside every weight, and sin which clings so closely, and let us run with endurance the race that is set before us, looking to Jesus, the founder and perfecter of our faith, who for the joy that was set before him endured the cross, despising the shame, and is seated at the right hand of the throne of God."

Focus on your life and what's ahead. Your lane. God knows what's in front of you, now commit to get over your obstacle.

I know what it's like to be afraid of the hurdles in front of you. I know what it's like to be afraid to move. Even knowing that God was in the boat with me and that Jesus rose from the dead, I still couldn't stop myself from going through the natural processes of being a human. I sat in front of my hurdle for so long until I finally had to admit what happened. And not only did it happen, it happened seven years ago.

"You been sitting in front of this thing for a long time. Are you ready to start back up running?" God asked me.

"Yeah, God, but I don't know how."

"Just have the courage to get over it. Get up, and get over it. And after you do that, Tommie, I want you to do it again. And after you do it again, I want you to do it faster the next time. And after you do that, I want you to go even faster. And before you know it, you'll be getting over it because it's who you are becoming: an overcomer."

Overcoming doesn't finally "happen;" it is a process of becoming. Again and again and again until overcoming isn't something you did, it's who you are. You didn't just overcome, you *are* an overcomer.

That is the end goal of endurance—becoming an overcomer. Enduring means you are on your way to overcoming. The end goal is not that you are forever an endurer, but that you become an overcomer!

If you're sitting in front of a hurdle, let me ask: have you considered that God might just be building an overcomer?

Chapter 13
THIS MAY BE MY LAST TIME
Cleats Off

Shortly after writing Deflated in Nashville, my father started experiencing kidney failure and I came home to help my family nurse him after he turned down hemodialysis. He fought a hard fought battle for nine months and we had some of our greatest times together in that time. Laughing. Singing. Telling stories. Mama's cooking.

On August 16, 2020, my biggest hero passed away at sixty-three-years-old.

I remembered our last conversation as I wheeled him to an ambulance that had come to take him to the hospital. He had just had a stroke and they needed to check his vitals.

"See ya later, son," he said.

"See ya later, dad," I said back.

Somehow, he knew that was the last time.

As I stood at his funeral, I silently cried beneath my sunglasses. To pass away from old age is one thing but my dad was still young.

Another hurdle, I thought.

Dad was my number one supporter through everything. He was always an up beat spark of life, and if there was any answer I needed to know, he had it like a walking encyclopedia. He was always the hardest worker in the room, never tolerated excuses, and knew how to find joy in the little things like singing before dinner.

My dad taught me how to be a good father.

When I was a boy, I remember getting ready to go fishing one day and my dad came to me and said, "Man, I can't teach you none of this stuff you doing. I can't do none of it. Nobody ever showed me. My dad never did anything for me. I don't know how to do it. But if this can get me more time with you and this is what you love, can you teach me how to fish?"

That right there changed my life. I'd see some of my friends' dads approach fatherhood with a "Well my dad never taught me!" attitude. But my dad turned the table. He had the guts to come and say, "I don't know how, but I'd love to learn if you can teach me."

Greatest of all, he constantly led our family toward Jesus. He built us up with God's word and sowed into us with love and wisdom. He knew how to lead.

Now, he was gone.

I felt like I was covered in scars.

My wife Ashley passed away from a brain aneurysm. That left a jagged wound that took years to heal. I still have the scar.

My daughter Thalia died of Sudden Infant Death Syndrome (SIDS). That ripped open a new wound and left a scar.

My kids nanny, Nanny B, had a fatal head-on car collision just last Christmas only a month or so after I wrote Deflated. That left a scar.

And now, my father battled his way through nine months on his way to heaven. That left another scar.

But there's a beautiful thing about scars: while they remind us where we were hurt, they also remind us how every new moment we have is a gift.

I'm reminded of a time during my very first start in the NFL when I started to sing in the tunnel. My father spent twenty years in the military and, like him, I was preparing for battle.

It was at Soldier Field Stadium, 7:00 pm kick-off and I could hear the roaring stadium just beyond the tunnel exit. Fifty-thousand fans or so thundered outside and adrenaline pulsed through my veins like electricity. I was wired. Sixty-two other players filled the tunnel with me, blue and orange jerseys on our backs, all of us locked and loaded for war. My brothers.

It was the third pre-season game of my first year in the NFL. August 27, 2004, and I was heading out with the starting lineup. We were facing off against the New Orleans Saints.

Anyone who's played pro-football knows that the third preseason game is the real deal. That's when the team locks in the players we're going to battle with before the real bullets start flying.

I'd already played two games in the NFL, but something struck me differently that day. I looked to my right and to my left and saw the faces of the men around me, and then out the end of the tunnel ahead of us. I thought about all the hard work I'd put in, all the early mornings and two-a-days, the late night workouts, runs, gym lifts, and rehab. I thought about the countless years of coaches yelling and encouraging me and remembered all the teachers who believed in me. I began crying. Thank God for the face mask.

I'd spent my whole life working toward this. Now, I was here. All the hard work I'd put in, all the moments I'd seen in my head since I was a kid, it all finally lined up: I was here! The dream had finally come through.

And yet, after today, it could all be gone.

I could snap a leg.

I could suffer a career-ending concussion.

I could get hit so hard that I black out, and never wake up.

This one game wasn't guaranteed, let alone the next game, the rest of the season, or the rest of my life. Every moment was a delicate gift. Every breath was worth savoring. Every day was worth making the absolute most of.

That was today.

Barely above a whisper, I started to sing an old spiritual that the slaves would sing before working:

This may be my last time

This may be my last time
This may be my last time
This may be my last time, I don't know

I learned it for the first time when I was seven years old, watching my daddy preparing to lead his troops into the desert storm in Bamberg, Germany, in 1991. He started giving my sisters and mother and I hugs like he wasn't coming back.

"Dad, when are you coming back?" I asked.

Dad always had a way with words. If I asked him where he was going his reply was, "To Heaven if I live right." If I asked him how he was doing he would say, "It doesn't matter. As long as the ground is underneath me and not on top, I got work to do."

But this day, Dad replied with a little melody in his voice, "This may be my last time. This may be my last time, I don't know."

No kid wants to hear that, so I told him, "Daddy, you will be back on my birthday! Don't worry, God told me."

Dad chuckled.

"If God told you, then I believe it."

On April 29, 1992, nearly a year later and coming up on my birthday, we got the call that all the soldiers were returning to base. Just like God told me. I was ecstatic. We set off to meet my dad, Sargent First Class (SFC) Harris, at the Bamburg airfield where what had to be about 300 buses awaited on the runway. My Father was the first man off the bus to give orders as the soldiers exited the busses and, with a final "At ease Solider," release them to their families.

When his job was done and I finally got to run into his embrace, I remembered the song he sang, and every day after that I heard Dad sing it at home or at church, I remembered him as he prepared to lead his troops into battle.

The song became my anchor in times of fear and doubt, and as I sang it in the tunnel before last preseason game, I let it's words fill me with strength.

"This may be my last time… This may be my last time… this may be my last time… it may be my last time, I don't know…"

The words soothed me and reminded me of the significance of this moment. It wasn't just another game, it was the game I had *right now*. I wasn't promised another. Was I ready to play this game like it was my last?

I had played with guys in college and high school who were better than me, and in the greatest game of their life, tore a knee or ACL, never to walk without crutches again or make it back on the field. I played against players who should have been NFL legends and who might have earned a place in the Hall of Fame, if not for sustaining a career ending injury. I'd had too many friends get hurt in and out of the game to miss the message: This may be your last time.

But that's not a reason to live in fear. The opposite, really. That's motivation to live every moment of every day with everything you've got.

This may be my last time, I don't know…

I continued to sing, and then I sang louder. And as I let the words add to the electric energy in the tunnel, I filled myself with their meaning.

Every game was an opportunity to leave it all on the field. Every breath was a chance to live all in. Every moment was a gift to be fully savored.

Savor Every Moment

Shortly after Ashley passed away, I had the opportunity to hike Mount Kilimanjaro in Tanzania with a few friends. It was one of the hardest things I've ever physically done and, at the same time, one of the most beautiful experiences of my life.

It was at around 11,000 feet that the wisdom of our guides really started to sink in. "Polepole," they kept telling us, which is Swahili for "Slow down." The reason for this was to acclimate to the altitude. With each new step, we had to get acclimated in order to climb higher or we would end up too sick with altitude sickness to go any further.

After my first night of labored breathing, I understood! You got to respect the climb or it will spit you out.

I started to wonder, where am I rushing in life's mountain? Where in life am I neglecting to take the time to acclimate? I learned that a sure way to pinpoint the answer is to look for places in your life where you're sick.

Is your marriage dry? Are your relationships with your kids strained? Is your work constantly filled with stress? If so, then the problem might be altitude sickness.

As we continued our climb, one step after the other, I worked to keep my head up. I noticed that when I was rushing my head was pointed to the ground, but when I slowed down, I was able to look up and observe the beauty around me. I was able to be grateful for being up here and having this opportunity to see the world from this view.

I learned that rushing the climb will not only make you sick, but it will also cost you the joy of the journey.

Where in life are you missing the beauty because you're in too big a hurry to look up? Where are you rushing? Where are you sick?

If you allow yourself the proper time to acclimate, your strength to finish the climb comes naturally. The same goes for life. If you can respect the journey of life and slow down, see people, and give people their flowers while they can smell them, everything seems to just come.

Slow down and allow yourself to acclimate, and even the hardest climbs are beautiful. Whatever moment you have in front of you slow down to taste it, and when I say taste it I mean have a seat and savor every moment believing the best is yet to come.

It's like the story I heard once about a young woman who was diagnosed with a terminal illness and had a short time left to live. As she met with her pastor about her memorial service, she told him which songs she wanted sung and what scriptures she would like read. And then, as they were just finishing up, the young woman suddenly remembered something very important to her.

"There's one more thing!" she said.

"What's that?" the pastor asked.

"It's very important," the young woman said with a sparkle in her eye. "I want to be buried with a fork in my right hand."

The Pastor looked at the young woman, confused. The woman smiled.

"In all my years of attending church dinners as a child," the woman started to explain, "I always remember that when the dishes of the main course were being cleared, someone would always lean over and say, 'Keep your fork.' It was my favorite part because I knew that something better was coming, like velvety chocolate cake or deep-dish apple pie! So, I just want people to see me there in that casket with a fork in my hand and I want them to wonder, 'What's with the fork?' Then I want you to tell them, 'Keep your fork, the best is yet to come.'"

Polepole, and savor every moment as you come to it. As you watch people move from this life to the next, don't let it scare you, let it remind you to keep your fork. After all, the best is yet to come.

Chapter 14
RESUME YOUR RACE

Cleats On

"Let's run, boys!"

I've lived under the rule of those words for most of my life. Running drills for Coach Marinelli in the NFL. Running laps for Coach Shipp in college. Running suicides for Coach Kenny in high school. Running sprints. Running relays. Running 5Ks. Running because Coach was mad. Running to increase speed. Running to build stamina. Running to warm up. Running for punishment. Running for training. Running for conditioning.

In all my running, I've felt the mythical "second wind" overtake my body more than once.

Ten minutes into a team 5K and I'd be dying. Dehydrated, cramping, and sore from my back to my butt and down both legs, I'd feel like heat exhaustion was on my doorstep. I couldn't breathe. Darkness was settling in. My vision was turning into sparkles. And then, just as I was about to collapse, BAM! It felt like I grew a third lung.

Things would start to change.

My strength would return full force and then some. My heavy panting would turn into strong breaths. My muscles would no longer feel fatigued, but rather, warmed up. I would feel stronger and faster than when I started, like I could keep going for hours.

So, what just happened? Is it magic? Not quit.

The second wind is a legit physiological phenomenon that occurs during strenuous activity after you have exerted most of your initial energy and strength. After a certain point, when you feel like they have run out of breath and yet continue to press on through the fatigue, your body's energy levels eventually rebound as if they suddenly found a new source of strength and your heavy breathing returns to a sustainable level.

So, what causes this?

Psychologists theorize that part of the second wind effect is due to endorphins being released like in a runner's high, but there's more to it than that.

Everyday, your body is constantly transferring the energy from carbohydrates, fat, and protein into a high energy molecule known as Adenosine Triphosphate (ATP) so it can be used to fuel your muscles. This transfer occurs with one of two processes: aerobic metabolism, which occurs with the presence of oxygen, or anaerobic metabolism, which occurs without the presence of oxygen. The type of metabolism that is used during physical activity is determined by the demand for energy and the availability of oxygen.

During the first few steps of exercise, your muscles are the first to respond to the change in activity level. Your lungs and heart do not react as quickly, however, and take time to increase the delivery of oxygen, so your muscles rely on the small amount of ATP that is stored in resting muscles. But that only provides energy for several seconds, and once the stored ATP is just about used up, the body resorts to another high-energy molecule known as creatine phosphate to produce more ATP. After about ten seconds, the stored creatine phosphate in the muscle cells are also depleted as well.

This puts your muscles in a tough place. With your brain still demanding motion and still no influx of oxygen from the lungs and heart to aid in the process of aerobic metabolism, the muscles must begin to produce ATP by anaerobic metabolism—without oxygen.

Your body can produce ATP very quickly with anaerobic metabolism, but this form of metabolism only uses glucose as its fuel source and, without oxygen present, the broken down glucose creates a waste byproduct: lactic acid.

As lactic acid continues to build up, our body grows tired and sluggish. Our breathing grows labored and heavy as our lungs try to catch up and repay the oxygen "debt" that our muscles generated by going into anaerobic metabolism, our body burns and aches, and every step feels heavier than the last.

But, as you continue to carry on, things eventually change.

After about ten to fifteen minutes for the average person, the increased labor of the heart and lungs start to pay off. The muscles finally start receiving the oxygen levels they need to resume aerobic metabolism and stop mass-producing lactic acid, your breathing levels out, your heart rate settles into its new pace, your body attains proper temperature and starts self-cooling through sweat rather than heavy breathing, and everything falls into equilibrium.

Physiologists theorize that this process of achieving oxygen equilibrium is primarily responsible for creating the anticipated "second wind."

I've come to think of the second wind as life's metaphor of hope. Why continue to run when, with every step, it seems to get harder? Your breathing is growing more and more labored, your heart feels like it's going to explode, your muscles burn, you feel like you're dying of heat, and you feel like your going to throw up? Because the second wind is coming.

It takes audacity to continue on in life with the expectation that your spirit will be renewed. I'm talking to the people who still believe God will show up and revive your breathing and keep you cool when life gets heated.

Isaiah 40:29-31 says it best: "He gives power to the faint, and to him who has no might he increases strength. Even youths shall faint and be weary, and young men shall fall exhausted; but they who wait for the Lord shall renew their strength; they shall mount up with wings like eagles; they shall run and not be weary; they shall walk and not faint."

If you will continue to run, God will revive you. He will cool you down when you're heated, he will clean out the toxins in your body, he will transform you from the inside out. He is leading you into your second wind, stronger and faster than ever before! But it requires a process of development to take effect, so keep running and remember that waiting time is not wasted time. The second wind is coming!

Stretching

I've been a big fan of Jamaican sprinter Usain Bolt since I first watched him take the 2008 summer Olympics by storm in Beijing, winning gold medals in both the 100m and 200m sprint and setting new world records for both. Before, he was just another runner. Afterward, he was universally recognized as the fastest man in history. He was the "PR" king—not of press releases, but of personal records. His goal wasn't the clout but to push himself to be the best he could be, and was just getting started.

On August 17, 2017, Usain Bolt was on the block for the last race of his career. I was watching it in real time. It was a 4X100 relay, and Bolt was positioned as the anchor for the last stretch.

"On your mark…"

The runners placed their backfoot against the starting block.

"Set…"

Their bodies lifted into starting position, tense like tigers ready for the kill.

BANG!

The first relay sprinters exploded off the blocks. 100 meters later, they passed their patons to their second leg. Then to their third. And then, the final leg, the anchor, where Usain Bolt was locked and loaded.

The race was down to the last 100 meters with Jamaica, Great Britain, and the United States in front. Driving the last leg home for the win was Bolt's speciality. He exploded off his block, took the patton, and then, just as he was digging for the finish line, he pulled up.

Halfway down the last 100 meters of his career, Bolt's body visibly cramped and he skipped on one leg to a halt in the middle of the track, falling to the ground in pain as the other runners flashed past him. Great Britain finished taking the lead over the United States and claimed the gold while Bolt's teammates rushed to his side. As they lifted Bolt to his feet and helped him limp across the finish, I nodded my head in memory of my own injury ten years ago and thought, "Your hamstring ripped. Sucks, man. Bet you didn't stretch enough."

I used to hate stretching. It was boring, painful, and did little to elevate my game as far as I was concerned. But after my injury, I learned a new appreciation for it.

After suffering through months of rehab, I not only have my masters in business but hamstrings, too, and one thing I know is that I could have saved myself a lot of pain and surgery if I had only stretched better before that fateful game. My hamstring rehab was the hardest rehab process I've ever had to endure, and it was primarily due to lack of flexibility.

In rehab, my physical therapist would push my leg everyday past the point I thought was full extension. Man, it hurt. But I learned how stretching promotes strength development in limbs at new extension extremes, sends blood flow to the closed off or injured areas in your body, and helps tight muscles become fully functional again.

It was painful, but it was necessary.

In the years after my time in the NFL, I've learned that rehab in life requires stretching as well.

When you've taken a big hit in life, it can hurt to just twitch your muscles, let alone bend your whole arm or leg. It can hurt to trust people again after you've had friends leave or take advantage of you. It can hurt to risk starting a business again after going bankrupt the first time. It can hurt to pursue your dreams again after having them crushed before. And in truth, if you tried to hurl yourself past the pain and do it again anyway, there's a good chance you could injure yourself even more.

Stretching is how you warm up your muscles before putting weight on them in order to avoid overloading them. It takes a little patience, but it keeps you from hurting yourself further with overextension.

How do you stretch in life? With dreams and prayer.

Stretching after an injury is not the same as chillin'. Sometimes, taking a break is important, but not once you decide you're ready to get back running. Stretching is not a passive activity. You also can't simply bend over as far as is comfortable and then stand up right again. Stretching requires you to go *past* the point of comfortability, and more, *hold* the position for an extended period of time.

In the wake of losing my wife and NFL career, my entire life felt hyperextended. My marriage was cut short like an amputated leg. My fatherhood muscle hurt every time I flexed it. My future stung to think about. The Super Bowl was painful to watch. The friendships that used to hold my life together like tendons were torn or tearing.

It took awhile before I was able to stand back up and run in life again. Long before I was ever able to talk about my story on stage, in a song, or in a book to help others, I spent countless hours stretching my heart with dreams and prayer.

What did I hope to see life look like again?

What were God's desires for me?

What did I want for my kids and family?

What was God teaching me?

What kind of work did I want to get into?

What did it mean to find peace in Jesus?

If it's taking you a while to come back from a pulled muscle too, I want you to remember that it's okay. Proper stretching takes time. I've watched some people go through loss and completely rebound afterward with emotionally charged impulses rather than heart-crafted desires, and they usually end up more lost and desperate than they were before.

Take your time. Dream, pray, and gently push yourself past your comfort zone.

If you need to forgive someone, start by stretching your forgiveness muscle by dreaming of what you want your relationship to eventually look like with them again and genuinely praying for them. Stretch your muscle first, and then put weight on it.

If you are going for a risk taker's decision for the second time, stretch your risk muscle by learning from other people, listening to and reading the stories of other people who have accomplished courageous feats, and praying for God's guidance and favor. Stretch your muscle to make sure it's warmed up, and then put weight on it.

In whatever it is, start with proper stretching, and then put weight on it. Stretching encourages blood flow and gets the muscle active without putting weight on it too soon.

Use your mind and prayer to start moving your mental and spiritual muscles past where you thought they could go before and stretch!

Overcomer

About a year ago, I found myself at a restaurant watching a track meet on TV. What caught my eye most was the hurdles race, where the track was filled with intentional obstacles to test the athlete's athleticism. And as I watched, I felt like God gave me a vision.

I was sitting down in front of a hurdle while sprinters were flying past me on either side. Six lanes full of people just running in open lanes. But from my view, I was sitting in a lane full of hurdles.

In my heart I asked, God, what is this? What does this mean?"

I felt his answer like a gentle whisper.

"Tommie, in your life, you've always compared your race to sprinters. 'Looks like they're going places faster and getting through things faster.' But I want you to fix your eyes straight ahead. And I want you to commit to your lane every day. Find your pace and keep it."

"What do you mean?" I asked.

"In order for your race to start moving forward again, you're going to have to commit daily to forgive yourself and stop comparing your life to others and to get over some things."

"But God, why do I have to get over some things and they're just sprinting?" Even sprinters at times have hurdles. I thought to myself Bolt getting hurt is his own hurdle; he has to learn how to get over his own obstacle.

"Because they're learning to sprint right now. Don't worry about them. Right now with you, I'm building something in you that's different."

"What's that?"

"I'm building an overcomer."

If you feel like your lane has hit you with obstacles and you're constantly comparing your life to people who are moving and you just feel like you're not, I'd consider that just maybe God is building an overcomer. And as an overcomer, your job is to start getting over some things.

"Yeah, but my dad wasn't there when I was little," you might say. You have to get over it so your race can continue.

"I was abused when I was little." You have to get over so your race can move.

"Yeah, I was cut from the team." Get over it.

"I was dropped from school." Get over it.

"I was fired and went broke." Get over it.

Life only continues when we decide to get over some things.

Why? Because it's your race. That's the only way it moves. God is building an overcomer in you! How do I know? Because if he wasn't, we wouldn't be having this conversation.

You gotta start getting over some things. I don't say that in a mean way, I'm saying it because your race will stagnate until you finally go address that thing that's been keeping you paralyzed. And once you address it, it's time to get over it.

Let's go. We got a race to run.

It might hurt. You might limp for a while. I know I did. You might be scared of tripping over another hurdle. You might not be as fast as the other runners yet and they'll keep flying past you for a while. It might take some time for you to get your stride back, but the question isn't if you can start out perfect, the question is, are you ready to start getting it back?

Remember, just like the prize race horse, make sure you put your blinders on everyday. Stick cotton in your ears and shut out the voice of the enemy. Your life is uniquely unlike any others. It's your race, not anyone else's. As the author of the book of Hebrews compels us in Hebrews 12:1-2, "Therefore, since we are surrounded by so great a cloud of witnesses, let us also lay aside every weight, and sin which clings so closely, and let us run with endurance the race that is set before us, looking to Jesus, the founder and perfecter of our faith."

Focus on your lane and getting over what's ahead of you. A wise runner never looks to the left or right during the race, just to the finish line. God knows what's in front of you, now commit to get over it it.

I know what it's like to be afraid of the hurdles in front of you. I know what it's like to be afraid to move. Even knowing that God was in the boat with me and that Jesus rose from the dead, I still couldn't stop myself from going through the natural processes of being a human. I sat in front of my hurdle for so long until I finally had to admit, it happened. And not only did it happen, it happened seven years ago.

"You been sitting in front of this thing for a long time. Are you ready to start back up running?" God asked me.

"Yeah God, but I don't know how."

"Just have the courage to get over it. Get up, and get over it. And after you do that, Tommie, I want you to do it again. And after you do it again, I want you to do it faster the next time. And after you do that, I want you to go even faster. And before you know it, you'll be getting over it because it's who you are becoming: an overcomer."

Overcoming doesn't finally "happen," it is a process of becoming. Again and again and again until overcoming isn't something you did, it's who you are. You didn't just overcome, you are an overcomer.

That is the end goal of endurance—becoming an overcomer. Enduring means you are on your way to overcoming. The end goal is not that you are forever an endurer, but that you become an overcomer!

Chapter 15
RENEWING

Cleats Off

It was March of 2021 and I was back in my old stomping grounds: Chicago, Illinois, home of the Bears. I'd made a deal with Tyson and Tinsley that if they did good on their grades we could go visit some friends and family there for spring break. They upheld their grades, so here we were, and I was as grateful as them for the reprieve.

We all needed a break. Especially me. I felt like I was under more pressure than I'd ever been in my life.

With crowds prohibited from gathering as a result of the COVID-19 pandemic, I'd been out of work as a motivational speaker for over a year. And that had left me tight on money.

The first time I really felt the finances closing in on me was last August after my father passed away. No one in my family had the money to pay for My Fathers funeral and they all thought I was still stacked, so the responsibility fell on me to fit the bill. But I wasn't stacked. I was barely making it.

After burying My father and speaking at his funeral, all I really wanted was a chance to simply be a child at my dad's funeral. But I didn't have the luxury. I was the man of the family now, and I had to step into the role.

I felt the lowest I'd ever felt. I thought all the other prior lows I had experienced in my life were my rock bottom, but now, I learned there was a level even deeper. Now, the only person I truly shared everything with was gone.

With tears in my eyes, I approached the funeral coordinator to pay the bill. My wallet felt like a worthless wad of cardboard in my hand. I tried to convince myself that maybe, after swiping every card and maxing out all my accounts, I would be close enough to the total that they would forgive the remaining balance.

My hand trembled as I reached for my first card, but before I could get it out, the lady stopped me.

"Mr. Harris, your bill has already been paid in full. Your friend Jack Brewer heard your father passed away and wanted to cover it."

I stood still for a moment, hand still trembling. Jack Brewer was a friend of mine from the league.

He paid the bill?

I could barely believe it.

Thank you Jack! I thought in my head. *Thank you God!*

Thank the Lord for small blessings. But still, my father was gone and my life was running on E.

My father had always been my rock in my life. He was my hero, my guide, my reminder of God's peace in the midst of the storm. A true soldier, both in the US army and for the Lord. In my heart I was devastated, but I didn't have the space and time to acknowledge it.

Get back in the action! Perform, T! You got this!

My mom needed me more than ever after losing her husband of forty-three years.

My kids needed me more than ever since the pandemic canceled their school and they were starting homeschooling.

My extended family needed me more than ever since the pandemic was taking a toll on their jobs and businesses.

Bills were piling up. Old friends no longer felt like friends but resources. I was trying to help the kids adjust to homeschooling. The pandemic made me feel distant from people at a time when all I wanted to do was share my story. I felt like the more I shared with others the more I healed. I know I'm not the only one who can attest to the toll that this global pandemic had on humanity.

Then, to top it all off, I was in the middle of writing this book.

I was expected to deliver on story pieces and lessons before certain deadlines, but for the first time in my life, I felt like everything I had once spoken about so passionately had dried up. My imagination was empty and my creativity felt forced.

Everyone needed my attention. My publisher, my kids, my mom, the boys I mentor, old teammates going through tough times—everyone needed me and I didn't have anything to give and the pressure made me feel like a dam getting ready to bust!

Like I said, as my kids and I arrived in Chicago for spring break, I was grateful for the reprieve. But even then I felt overwhelmed, and deep down, I knew what I needed: help.

I was still too prideful to admit it to anyone but myself, but I needed another person's help. The money was not important. I always believed God would provide all of my needs. But what happens when you start becoming spiritually bankrupt? I needed a hand up not a hand out. Someone to talk with, to open up with, to share my burden with. A true friend.

But how do you ask for help when you're the one everyone goes to for help?

In a sorry attempt to relieve my stress, I called up a few teammates hoping for a blast of nostalgia. Nothing too deep, just a little reminder of "how things used to be."

One of those guys was Matt Forte. He was one of my closest friends and former teammates in Chicago, and more, we used to be "couple" friends: Ashley and I used to go out with Matt and his wife. Matt was in town so we met up and reminisced about the good old days. But still, all I could do was think about my present situation.

How did you end up here Tommie? What did you not see? What could you have done better? Where did you make the wrong turn?

As we continued to talk, I started to see my real enemy: my inner me. The part of me that refused to ask for help and continued to hold onto the past. The part of me that continued to live in the voice of "would of could of should of."

Eventually, Matt and I prayed, hugged, and peaced out.

I felt a little better after touching base with Matt, but was still missing the depth of release I really needed. I needed a shoulder to cry on and a friend to talk to, but I wasn't good at it and didn't know how to ask. It felt awkward being on this side of the ball. I was used to being the guy with all the answers, the guy other's came to for comfort and help.

Now, it was the other way around.

But God knew what he was doing. He was sculpting me like a piece of clay. He had shaped me in many ways throughout my life with his hands and chisel, and now, he was going to work on one of my greatest fractures: my pride.

On a mission to to find help, I decided to call another trusted friend: Double A or "Dub," better known as Spice Adams. One of my closest friends who had been worried about me but I had been hiding from. I told him I needed to tell him the truth.

"Hey Dub, you busy? Kids and I are here in Chicago. I need to talk, come on brother I'll be here."

As the kids played outside I was rehearsing my lines like a college kid fresh out, getting ready for the first big interview. I did not know how to do this. This sure was unfamiliar territory for me but I wanted to be free.

We hit the weights for a workout and began talking a little while we lifted. I still couldn't get out what I really needed to get out. We finished the bench and moved to boxing. I still couldn't get it out.

"Great work out," we both said.

Still nothing.

We sat around and talked about our kids for awhile.

Come on, T!

But I couldn't.

We shook hands, hugged, and said our goodbyes. And I never said what I was really there for. "Help." Not financially, but just to know I wasn't alone.

Let's Eat!

As I prepared for bed that night, I worked to hide the tears in my eyes from my kids. We were staying with my sister-in-law Dana, Ashley's sister, and I was staying on a couch in the living room. I managed to keep my emotions together on the surface, but inside, I was a wreck.

Why you always gotta be okay? You're not perfect, remember? You gotta say something to someone! You can't do this alone. You can't help others if you don't let others helps you, Tommie!

As I wrestled with my thoughts on my sister-in-laws couch, a still, small voice whispered in my heart, "You better get to New Life in the morning like your life depends on it."

I sat in that thought for a moment.

What? I haven't been to New Life church in years...

New Life was the church I attended when I first arrived in Chicago as a rookie with the Bears. Pastor John Hannah was one of the mightiest men of God I knew and was one of the few pastors I had ever seen cry on stage. I always found my way there for Thursday night Bible study and, when the games schedule allowed, Sunday morning service even if it was only for half the time. Pastor Hannah's heart was genuine and the spirit of the Lord was palpable in that place. Somehow, it had always felt like home.

God I don't know where to start, I prayed. *I haven't talked to these people in forever. I don't know who to call.*

I was scared to go. But the feeling that I *must* go only continued to grow stronger, and finally, I couldn't resist it any longer.

Okay. But if you want me there, you have to help me get me there.

New Life used to hold services in King Highschool at 46th and Drexel back when I was a regular, but since then, had started construction on a new, huge auditorium building to move into. I knew one of my friends, CJ, was closely affiliated with the construction job, and so I pulled out my phone to call him. It was midnight and we hadn't talked in ages, but I felt like I was supposed to call him.

Here goes nothing...
One ring.
See God, I told you everybody has their own stuff! I don't want to be one of those people who weighs everyone else down with his problems.
Second ring.
This is stupid, I'm hanging up. It's midnight and I told you, there's no way he's gonna—
Just as I was about to end the call, the line clicked and an excited voice interrupted my argument with God.
"What's up brother! How are you?!"
Wow. Okay, God, I'll work on my patience, I thought.
"Hey bro. I'm good. I'm actually in town right now. I was trying to come to church tomorrow morning and..."
"Yo, let me know where you're at!" he interrupted again. "We're having service in the new building for the first time this Sunday and they are only letting so many people in due to the COVID restrictions. Text me your pin. I'll be there to pick you up at nine for the ten o'clock service!"

The next morning, I was up and ready to go at 7:30.
Anyone who knows me knows that I am *not* a morning person, but this morning, I was amped. As I walked into the church building, the energy of God's people filled me with fresh fire. There was a spiritual fragrance that kindled my appetite for truth like a vagrant wanderer who has just smelled fresh bread for the first time in years. If God's word was Food, then I was starving!

I felt like a kid waking up early on Thanksgiving morning to the smell of Momma's cooking in the kitchen. Sweet potato pie, cranberry salad, turkey and dressing with gravy, and homemade bread! Except, this morning, God was making the feast. I didn't know all the ingredients, but I knew I loved his cooking.

As I anticipated church and listening to Pastor Hannah's message that morning, I seriously could not wait for the hope and power I always found contained in the truth of God's word. I hadn't been this hungry for God's word in years, and it felt great to have my appetite back.

Let's EAT!

CJ and I made our way through the back of the church, looking for Pastor Hannah. One of the church armorbearers wanted to surprise him that I was here before the service started, but yet again, that still, small voice spoke in my head.

"Tommie, this is not why I have you here. Stay focused."

I listened and understood. I didn't want to greet, I wanted to eat!

After a few minutes of searching and checking Pastor Hannah's backstage room with no luck, we gave up. "Okay, God. Thanks for keeping me focused." I chuckled in my heart as we worked our way through the overly excited crowd to our seats.

I've always been one to stay out of the way when it comes to being in church services. When offered a front row seat, I always asked to sit in the back or to be hidden behind the curtain. I wasn't a fan of being a "celebrity christian" and didn't want the attention on me more than anyone else while I was at church. But on this particular day, I was grateful to be front and center. Today, I was starving for the word. A front row seat was like receiving an invitation to God's banquet and he was doing the cooking.

Due to the COVID restrictions we were instructed not to remove our masks, which worked out great for me because it allowed me to stay discrete even while sitting up front.

As the service began, I was swept over with a sense of joy and all I could do was thank God for hearing my distressed heart and speaking to me. I'd spent so much time worrying and caring for other people's hearts that I had forgotten I had one and that I needed love and care also.

"Tommie, you can't pour from an empty cup Bubba," I felt the still, small voice say.

I couldn't see it in the moment, but what I soon realized was that part of the reason I felt so exhausted was because I had not been *eating*. I was pouring out, I was constantly giving of myself and speaking into others and helping others through their stuff, but I wasn't taking anything in. I was trying to recover from an injury but I was neglecting my *diet!*

Just like your physical diet determines the strength your body has to perform, so does your mental, emotional, and spiritual diet. All the exercise in the world won't help much if you're not eating right, and I hadn't been eating at all.

You have to take in nourishment in order to put out strength. Over the years I've learned that What you fill yourself up with determines how you will feel about yourself. It would be Like pumping 87 octane into a Lamborghini. It wouldn't get very far. What are you running on ?

I was empty.

Another Victory

As the service began and the energy of worship filled the room, I joined my voice to the chorus of other singers and embraced the peace and joy of God's presence like a gasp of fresh air. It had been too long.

Then, Pastor Hannah took the stage.

"Can everyone say, 'and another victory.'"

The crowd echoed it back.

"Come on, I need to hear those words come out of your mouth. And another victory! And another victory! And another victory!"

The audience was wild as Pastor Hannah continued to stir the room. Finally, he dove into the scriptures and the story of David, unfolding the meaning of each of David's three anointings on his way to becoming king of Israel.

His first anointing occurred when the prophet Samuel anointed David as a twelve-year-old boy. But what happened after that? Did he become king right away? Nope. He went back to shepherding sheep.

"How you gonna anoint someone at twelve and not give them the seat?" Pastor Hannah asked. "Listen, just because you're anointed doesn't mean it's your season yet!"

The second anointing occurred when the men of Judah came and anointed David as king over Judah at around thirty-years-old.

"But I thought I was gonna get all of Israel!" Pastor Hannah said, imagining David's thoughts. "'You mean to tell me I waited from the time I was twelve to thirty to only get a tribe?' Yep."

The third anointing occurred when all the elders of Israel came to David at thirty-seven and finally anointed him king over all of Israel.

"God, why do you slow stuff down? Why did you anoint David at twelve and then make him wait until he was thirty? What's all these gaps? 'But I'm anointed to do it!' Anointed means that God has seen your heart. But character is acquired. God says, 'I can give you the oil, but I gotta give you some space to build your character.'" (2:36:20)

That's what endurance is all about. Endurance is building up who you are—your character.

"Pay attention to your victories. And another victory. And another victory. And another victory. I don't have it all yet, but I have another victory. I don't have it all together! But I have another victory. *I don't have it all yet,* but I have another victory!"

Then, Pastor Hannah leveled with the church.

"Allow me to have a transparent moment. Building this new building has been the hardest season of my life. I've been hit, kicked, spit on, cussed out, feelings crushed. The stress began to affect my body negatively. Some days, I felt depressed. There were people who I wanted to celebrate with me but they wouldn't celebrate. I realized I was becoming weak and looking to man rather than God for validation, but I demanded to live!"

Man. Even pastors go through it, I thought.

"So I decided I needed to go see a counselor. And as I prayed God would order my steps, he gave me a sponsorship. Means that somebody was gonna pay for me to go! I visited this counselor and this man began to help me embrace my heart issues. The counselor told me he needed me to embrace my pain. My hurt. Everything I'd been through. Then he said, 'Now ask yourself, what am I going to do with this? It can either kill you, or it can make you stronger!'"

I listened intently and continued to lean in.

"(2;45;30) Does anybody have a track record? Of times God was on your side? It wasn't just one and done. No, you have a track record of victories! And then another victory! And then another! Your prayer life has gotten better. Your patience has gotten better. Your endurance has gotten better! Come on here! Stop complaining to God for what's not better and praise God for what is! Is everything perfect? No! But is it still like it used to be? Far from it, and for that I give God glory! Another victory! Yep, that should have taken me out, but I won again! Another victory! Do you still believe what he told you? Tommie, do you still believe the vision he gave you? He didn't give it to nobody else—he put it in you! Do you still believe the words that you once spoke?"

My mind took a double take.

What? Did he just say my name?

"Look at that screen. 2 Samuel 5:2. It says, 'In the past while Saul was over us, you—you, you, you!—you were the one who led Israel into and out of battle!' David, you have a track record. We're coming to you because we've seen you win victories! We've seen you overcome some stuff, *Tommie Harris,* that would have made the average person break. Who buries their wife after they just had a child and still believes God is God? Ooo, Tommie Harris! What did you speak over yourself when you were young? You have won victory after victory after victory!"

No denying it this time. He was speaking directly to me.

"Stop! Don't focus on your battles right now, focus on your victories! Worship God right now for another victory! You are weak, you are tired, and the enemy thought that he had taken your mind, but God is giving it back! Worship God for another victory! Listen to me, you cannot do this on your own. You cannot do this without God! Worship God for another victory!"

As the service continued to build and then concluded, I let the message impact my thinking. No, I didn't have the final victory yet, but I did have another victory, and another, and another.

A lesson I'm still learning is not to despise the process. Like so many, I want God to finish his work in me *now!* I want to be healed *now!* God, can't it all be over *now?*

But what I'm learning is that while the final victory over all my pain and inner demons has not yet come, I can still rejoice in the victory in front of me and the victories he's given me so far. The final victory may not come until the very end, but every battle won on the way there is what will eventually win the war.

God hasn't brought you to the final victory yet but he has brought you to another victory! You're not finished enduring yet but you are stronger! The war is not over yet but this battle is won! And that is to be celebrated.

Don't despise your victories.

Sometimes, we forget. We forget the victories we have, we forget how far we've come, we forget what the Lord has taught us along the way, we forget how to be free from the pain and regret we lived in. That's okay. All that means is that we have to be relentless to remember.

That's the process of being refined like gold. As the apostle Peter writes in 1 Peter 1:6-7, "In this you rejoice, though now for a little while, if necessary, you have been grieved by various trials, so that the tested genuineness of your faith—more precious than gold that perishes though it is tested by fire—may be found to result in praise and glory and honor at the revelation of Jesus Christ."

By everything you've been through, God is making pure gold out of you.

Gold isn't refined without fire.
Overcomers aren't made without hurdles.
Champions aren't named without battles.
Be patient with the process of what God is doing.

After the service, Charlie and I attacked Pastor Hannah backstage with hugs. I hadn't seen him in years. We swapped stories and brought each other up to speed. I was about to leave when Pastor Hannah stopped me for one more minute.

"Tommie, I feel like I'm being led to tell you this: just like someone paid for me to go to counseling while we were building this church, someone is about to pay for you to go to counseling. They're going to pay it in full. And when they offer it to you, you need to accept it. You gotta be willing to ask for help and lean on others. Can't pour out if you never get filled up."

Counseling? Really?

But the more he talked about it, the more my pride began to tip, until finally, like God pulled the last block in a game of Jenga, it all fell down. Every little piece of doubt, loneliness, self-sabotage, un-forgiveness, and arrogance all began to scatter.

I thought of myself like I was in the seat of a crashing airplane. The flight attendant's warning continued to play in the speakers, "Everyone, please put your own oxygen mask on before assisting others!" But as I continued to help others and make sure they were good, I also continued to neglect my own oxygen mask.

But no longer. I was ready to breathe.

Wear Your Scars Like Medals

Leaving church, I couldn't go back to how I was before. Hiding my pain. Keeping up a look. Pretending I was fine. I'd learned vulnerability many times before and, more than likely, I would have to learn it many times again, but I refused to be discouraged by the fact that I was growing. I remembered Pastor Hannah's word: "And another victory."

As I climbed in my car, I called my friend Dub who I had worked out with the other day. I wanted to tell him the truth I had been too afraid to tell him then. That I needed help.

I didn't want to call him. I didn't know what to say. It was uncomfortable. But the words of my defensive line coach Rod Marinelli echoed in my head from the days of training on the Chicago Bears field: "Get comfortable being uncomfortable."

I found his contact and hit call.

"Yo!" Dub said, answering the phone.

"Dub, what's up bro."

"Not much," he said, then after a moment, "You doing okay?"

The moment of truth was here. No backing out this time.

"I'm not doing well bro. I need to get help. I can't think straight, I'm traumatized, and I feel like I'm falling apart. I need a TV timeout."

We laughed at that. The networks always took a commercial break whenever there was a timeout on the field. For us, that meant no spotlight and no cameras, just coach and the huddle.

"Seriously," I continued, "I need a counselor or someone to talk to. I need to get away for awhile and I'm not at capacity to do it for myself. I need help, bro. I feel like I'm…"

Before I could finish explaining myself, he interrupted.

"Bro! You won't believe this. I just got off the phone with someone who was telling me about this place where he helps retired athletes with mental and physical recovery. It's a dope place to get away and reset for a while. I'll call them for you and hit you right back."

The next morning he called back.

"It's done!" Dub yelled into the phone. "And get this, it's all paid for! They're gonna take care of you. "It's called PURE recovery outside of LAX. Go get right, bro!"

Tears filled my eyes as I thought about how God always has someone there for you. Most of the time, when we feel alone, it's not because no one cares but because we're afraid to reach out. That's how the devil wants to keep us: prideful, puffed up, self-sufficient, liars. Because that's how he can keep us isolated. I guess that's why the apostle Paul encourages us to "bear one another's burdens." (Galatians 6:2)

I don't have to be perfect before I run to God's arms, I thought. God knows I am a mess. He knows we're all a mess. But in him, we are being made new. Not fixed—made *new!*

Finally, I remembered again, "For God so loved the world that he gave his only begotten son for a beautiful mess like me." (John 3:16, Tommie Harris version)

I arrived in Los Angeles for the PURE retreat on May 5. Like Jesus who consistently sought solitude in the mountains to pray, so was I.

The following weeks were full of reflection, conversations with God, and time for silence and solitude intermixed with group discussions and one-on-one therapy sessions. Even as I was healing, I was able to have conversations with the other people there who were going through stuff and help them as well. I heard some stories about wounds I had not experienced, but I could still relate to the pain. An ouch is an ouch!

The more we shared, the more we healed. It was crazy sharing a house with some of the most powerful men I'd ever met and yet, we were each learning to replace our authority with vulnerability. I was tired of hiding my pain and everyone else was tired of hiding theirs.

What I didn't expect was that, one of those days, my natural bent to help others would rub my counselor the wrong way.

"What is it with you?" my therapist asked after one of our group discussions. I was seated on a couch in her office with the ambient sound of ocean waves crashing in the background.

I looked back, confused.

"You always have to have something deep and profound to say. You speak and everyone listens and just bows down to you like your God or something. Like you're the wisest person in the world. You make others feel like you're superior over them and they're inferior to you."

I thought about it for a moment.

"It sounds to me like that's a personal problem you have, not a problem with me."

"Don't give me that! You wear your scars like they're a badge of honor or something."

The moment those words left her mouth, something clicked in me. Something came full circle. Something made sense.

That's right. My scars are medals.

"Ma'am, when my father served in the army, he wore his medals proudly. Do you know why? Because they inspired the world, they honored the fallen, and most importantly, they reminded him of what he's been through. 'I made it. And if I can make it through that, I can make it through anything.' That's what my story is to me. I wear my scars like medals because I'm a soldier in the army of the lord, and if I've made it this far, I want to exemplify to others they can too. And I wear them because I want to remind myself, 'If you've made it this far, you can keep going.' So you bet that I wear my scars proudly. My father did, my savior did, and so will I."

That's my stance now, and I challenge you with it. Everywhere you go, wear your scars like medals. Revelation 12:11 tells us, "they have conquered him by the blood of the Lamb and by the word of their testimony," and I am decided that if my testimony holds power, I will not be afraid of it.

You don't have to be afraid or ashamed of your scars. Let the world see. Own 'em. You never know who might need to see them. Let your healing scars give others hope for their open wounds.

You feel lost in the darkness? Then let your life be the light everyone else is looking for.

Wear your scars like medals! Let them inspire others, honor those who have fallen, and remind you daily that the God who has brought you this far will never leave you nor forsake you. Wear 'em proudly! Let them boast the renewing God is doing.

You'll never be the same again, but if you can endure, you will be new. Like a potter working clay, God is making a new thing out of you. Your story is bigger than just you—others are watching. So wear your medals and let God use your endurance to not only renew you but the hearts of those around you!

And risk it on one turn of pitch-and-toss,
And lose, and start again at your beginnings
And never breathe a word about your loss;
If you can force your heart and nerve and sinew
To serve your turn long after they are gone,
And so hold on when there is nothing in you
Except the Will which says to them: 'Hold on!'

If you can talk with crowds and keep your virtue,
Or walk with Kings—nor lose the common touch,
If neither foes nor loving friends can hurt you,
If all men count with you, but none too much;
If you can fill the unforgiving minute
With sixty seconds' worth of distance run,
Yours is the Earth and everything that's in it,
And—which is more—you'll be a Man, my son."

In conclusion, remember God's promise painted throughout the breadth of scripture:

If you can endure, I will make you new again, my child.

Conclusion
IF

Over the years, I have often returned to a poem by Rudyard Kipling entitled *If.* It has served me many times as an anchor in the storm, a glimpse of hope in the fray of battle, a reminder of God's hand in the coldness of night. I pray it can serve you as it has me.

"If you can keep your head when all about you
Are losing theirs and blaming it on you,
If you can trust yourself when all men doubt you,
But make allowance for their doubting too;
If you can wait and not be tired by waiting,
Or being lied about, don't deal in lies,
Or being hated, don't give way to hating,
And yet don't look too good, nor talk too wise:

If you can dream—and not make dreams your master;
If you can think—and not make thoughts your aim;
If you can meet with Triumph and Disaster
And treat those two impostors just the same;
If you can bear to hear the truth you've spoken
Twisted by knaves to make a trap for fools,
Or watch the things you gave your life to, broken,
And stoop and build 'em up with worn-out tools:

If you can make one heap of all your winnings